Patronage and Poverty
in the Tobacco South
Louisa County, Virginia, 1860–1900

.

Patronage and Poverty in the Tobacco South

Louisa County, Virginia, 1860–1900

By Crandall A. Shifflett

The University of Tennessee Press

Knoxville

PUBLICATION OF THIS BOOK WAS SUPPORTED BY A GRANT FROM THE

National Endowment for the Humanities

.

Library of Congress Cataloging in Publication Data
Shifflett, Crandall A.
 Patronage and poverty in the tobacco South.
 Bibliography: p.
 Includes index.
  1. Louisa County (Va.)—Economic conditions.
 2. Louisa County (Va.)—Social conditions.   3. Social classes—Virginia—Louisa County—History—19th century.
 I. Title.
 HC107.V82L727   305.5'09755'465   82-6996

 ISBN 0-87049-359-0   AACR2

TO MY
Mother
AND THE MEMORY OF MY
Father

·

Contents

·

Illustrations

.

FIGURES

TABLES

Preface

.

My family has not always been poor. They are not poor now. They were not even poor when they came to this country as Scotch-Irish immigrants and squatted on the crest of the Blue Ridge mountains in Virginia, eventually lending the family name to a section of the mountains called Shiffletts' Hollow. There they farmed for several generations until the 1930s, when the federal government decided to build a road through the mountains for tourists. My great-grandfather's land lay in the path of what was to become Skyline Drive. He could not prove legal claim, so the family was dispossessed and went from Blue Ridge riches to Blue Ridge rags. Grandfather and father became tenants and sharecroppers for others in the mountains before finally leaving for the farms and mills of the Virginia Piedmont and another kind of poverty. Both my mother and father spent a lifetime trying to escape poverty before finally bringing their family a modicum of hard-won security. I grew up, not in Louisa County, but in neighboring Madison County. Yet Louisa held a special fascination for me: here was a once-rich slaveholding county rumored in my youth to be one of the "poorest counties around." Louisa's history seemed to parallel the life of my own family. There were other mysteries. Why did so many labor for so few for so little, and how had this state of affairs come about? And why did "they" seem to accept it? Years later these questions urged me toward a study of the social structure of the rural South. Louisa County seemed a good place to begin.

Louisa was attractive in other ways. The cotton culture has received much attention, while the tobacco culture has been ignored. Tobacco did not dominate Louisa's agriculture, but it was the basic cash crop for farmers until the 1880s, when largeholders moved into dairying and grass farming. Tobacco is a labor-intensive crop, and consequently Louisa had in its population a black majority, which lasted into the twentieth century.

Still other infuences molded this study of Louisa. A number of years ago, I began to read social histories of New England towns and studies of change and continuity in peasant societies of England, France, Italy, Spain, Brazil, and Mexico.[1] These studies stirred my interest in social history and alerted me to potential forces of change and transformation in the rural South. Most of them were intimate local studies. Gradually, I became convinced of the value of the community study as an ideal approach to historical questions I wanted to raise.

Louisa County represents no southern county statistically, of course, but it is representative of the processes of social change which affected nearly all southern counties during this period.[2] Dominated numerically by slaves, who in 1860 composed 62 percent of the population; governed by planters with accumulations of slaves and tobacco lands; jolted by the Civil War and the certainty forever of a guaranteed supply of labor; crippled by the destruction of the war and after it by the refusal of freedmen to work under the conditions offered by the planter class; and guided by a past of caste and class distinctions, Louisa County in these ways was the South. In addition, like other southern counties, it sought a substitute for slave labor, struggled to reconstruct itself, and failed to end class rule and racial subordination.

Of crucial importance in Louisa was patronage capitalism, whereby the means of production and distribution were privately owned but where no free market in labor actually functioned. After 1865, in the period typically called the "Emancipation Period," this system of patronage emerged in Louisa County and shaped the economic and political life of the county. Broadly conceived, it was a system of class and race control which led to rural poverty and perpetuated racism. As an economic system, patronage was another form of capitalism, not a fundamental deviation from it, just as slavery may be and has been seen as a distinct form of capitalism.[3] Under both slave and patronage capitalism, the position of capital remained essentially unchanged. Both slaveowners and patrons monopolized means of production and distribution and attempted to profit from their monopoly, whether by slave sales or breeding or by generating a surplus of new capital for investment. It was labor that underwent a fundamental change, not capital.

The essential difference between slave and patronage capitalism (and between both and free labor capitalism) was the changed position of labor. Under slavery, labor was capital; under patronage, labor was a commodity which planters still needed but no longer owned. Now they had to pay for it, bargain for it and the terms of its use, and recognize that it had rights under the law. Thus, it is labor which needs more attention, especially its new relationship to capital and the nature and meaning of this new relationship for the entire social order.

Patronage differed from the paternalistic system of slavery, as described by Eugene D. Genovese,[4] again because of the change in the position of labor. Patronage was not practiced to justify a labor system in moral terms, as Genovese has shown was the case with paternalism, because labor was legally free after the Civil War, and capitalism had not been declared immoral as the slave labor system had. Also, unlike paternalism, patronage capitalism had no compelling economic motivation to regard the well-being of labor. Indeed, expenditures for medical care, food, clothing, or shelter were no longer capital investments but instead were a part of the commodity costs of labor, and the incentive was to keep them as low as possible. Thus, patronage grew out of an entirely different set of goals and circumstances than those which shaped the slave economy.

Patronage capitalism differed from northern free labor capitalism, once more because of the unique position of southern labor. Unlike northern tenants, former slaves of Louisa were nearly destitute of the productive factors of agriculture. Theirs was not a poverty of land, which by itself cannot produce anything for the smallholder, but a poverty of oxen, horses, mules, scythes, rakes, hoes, plows, cultivators, mowers, and numerous other implements needed to transform land into a source of income and support. They had never needed to own them because the master had supplied them. Now, as legally free farmers, they found themselves shut off from these factors, and access to them required freedmen to bargain with local landowners. Although labor contracts, crop liens, and deeds of trust allowed destitute laborers to make a living, each agreement also bound them ever more tightly to their patrons. Soon, "free labor" became a hollow phrase, unlike what was meant in the North by the term. When the able-bodied and ambitious attempted to flee to nearby cities to escape the tentacles of patronage capitalism, federal policy and state laws restricted the movement of labor, again unlike anything faced by northern tenant farmers. Northern and western farmers were not rich and they had their mortgages, but few began without some means of production or at such slender levels of independence. None faced legal restrictions on their free movement.

After a brief survey of Louisa's economic history up to 1860, chapter one examines economic developments in the postwar period, compares Louisa's agricultural progress with other counties of the South and West, discusses the role of the Civil War as a factor in the county's agricultural decline, and describes the social structure in terms of the distribution of land and personal property holdings. Changes in the distribution of wealth between 1860 and 1900 receive detailed attention. Unlike many who have studied the period after the Civil War using a broad brush to paint the economic picture of the South in terms of regional trends, I have focused on the local, even personal, effects of economic change. From this perspective, it is obvious that land as a barometer of wealth and a source of economic mobility has been overemphasized to the exclusion of other factors of production.

Chapter two brings together landlords and tenants, elaborates capital-labor relationships which emerge from the crucible of the Emancipation Period, and distinguishes them from master-slave relationships as described by Eugene D. Genovese. I try to show that the paternalistic relationships of slavery gave way to what I have called "patronage capitalism" or, more broadly, "a system of patronage." According to C. Vann Woodward, slavery, poverty, race and class distinctions together with defeat on the battlefield constitute the "burden of southern history." Woodward makes it clear, however, that race and class distinctions have not been distinctly southern; indeed, during the Emancipation Period, they were characteristically American qualities.[5] Nevertheless, racial antipathy and economic inequality waned in the North in the twentieth century but continued to characterize the South. It is the question of the persistence of these distinctions in the South which this chapter addresses.

Chapter three is devoted to the laboring class and the conditions of labor in Louisa. It also shows the reaction of farm laborers to the immiseration produced by the patronage system. Although the evidence is not extensive, Louisa's clients did resist their economic subjugation, especially by migrating to nearby cities to seek alternative sources of work.

The next chapter deals with the attempts of Louisa's patron elite to restore their profits and demonstrates their responsiveness to the profit incentive. Worker resistance, a growing urban demand for dairy and poultry products, and the potential of grass farming to replenish the soil encouraged Louisa's large landholders to shift to more capital-intensive farming.

Chapter five unfolds the politics of patronage. Local politics took on renewed importance for Louisa's economic elite after the Civil War. The loss of slave wealth threatened the economic status of once-comfortable slaveowners. The Union government was determined to prevent former slaveowners from regaining political control of the statehouses. Louisa's former slaveowners reacted to the threats to their economic and political hegemony by taking firm control of local government and directing its affairs in their best interests.

Faced with misery and want and a selfish government, poor Louisans finally turned to their own households and families for support. In the changing composition of Louisa households over the life cycle of the family, the reader is brought face to face with the role of the family in a marginal economy. In patterns of marriage, birth, and death, the pernicious effects of the patronage system and the poverty it bred may be seen. At the same time, another story emerges of heroic struggles and the impressive resilience of the institution of the family. Whole families worked to make a living and perhaps in this way many black families were able to acquire enough to purchase small plots of land. These are the topics of chapter six.

Chapter seven draws some conclusions about the roots of poverty on the basis of the evidence in Louisa County. Poverty was the result of economic, political, racial, and demographic factors.

Just as this study was nearing completion, a debate erupted over the Emancipation Period. Economic historians, commonly called "econometricians" or "cliometricians," confronted historians who bring a Marxist perspective to their study of this period. The debate has been at times heated.[6] The issues are too complex to be treated in any detail here but will be given some attention in the Bibliographical Essay at the end of this book. To those who read it last, it should be clear that I have profited greatly from the debate and that I find weaknesses in both schools of thought. Cliometricians ignore the social and political bases of the economic order. They attempt to explain the history of the period only in terms of factors which are measurable, like income, capital flow, output, labor efficiency, or return on investment. Race and class distinctions, the forces of history, or political exigencies have to be ignored, blinked, or appended. Marxist social historians move beyond economic determinism to account for the economic stagnation of this period in terms of the social origins of the planters, whom they cast in the role of anticapitalists. Their argument does not explain why postwar planters became immune to the profit incentive, which was also a part of their social origins and which guided them as slaveowners. Moreover, in spite of their emphasis on class and class analysis, the Marxist historians give surprisingly little attention or credit to the laboring class and the dynamics of class cleavage. Both schools of thought present inexplicable discontinuities in southern history between slavery and the Emancipation Period.

This study attempts to provide a general theory of continuity and change in the South with poverty at center stage. The setting is Louisa County. The time is 1860–1900, as the county gropes for an alternative to slave society. The subjects are landlords and tenants acting as patrons and clients. Their script is the patronage system. The heroes and heroines are men, women, and children acting as families to combat the pernicious effects of racism and classism.

ACKNOWLEDGMENTS

I am pleased to acknowledge the assistance of many colleagues in writing this book. The late Edward E. Younger of the University of Virginia is largely responsible for my being in the field of history. His guidance and encouragement meant much to me as a graduate student. I am disappointed not to be able to share this moment with him but thankful for all he did for me. Josef J. Barton, now of Northwestern University, kindled my interest in social history while he was at Virginia. He has read and criticized my work many times and provided a model for me in his own broad-ranging scholarship. I owe to him my appreciation for social theory, comparative history, and the community study. Tom G. Kessinger shared with me his knowledge of family and community history from his own fine work in rural India.

Other colleagues have helped me to sharpen my argument during later stages of the book. Don H. Doyle of Vanderbilt University spent generous amounts of time criticizing my argument. Vernon Burton of the University of Illinois took time away from his own work to read my manuscript and offer valuable suggestions, too. As social historians with a deep understanding of the South, both understood what I was trying to say. A. Roger Ekirch, my colleague at Virginia Polytechnic Institute and State University, was a constant source of good advice and always open to my frequent visits to his office to discuss particular points. Robert Goldberg of the University of Utah read parts of the manuscript and offered helpful suggestions.

I have benefited greatly from institutional support. My graduate study would have been a great financial burden had it not been for the GI bill, which has made education affordable for thousands who otherwise would not be able to attend college. The history department at the University of Virginia provided additional fellowship support and a valuable instructorship in my final year of graduate study. The history department at Virginia Tech provided a reduced teaching load at a critical point. The staffs at the National Archives, especially James D. Walker, Alderman Library at the University of Virginia, and Virginia State Library, especially Joe Brent Tarter, eased my access to materials and pointed me toward useful sources of information. Dean Agee and the staff at the Louisa County Courthouse cheerfully answered my numerous questions and gave me complete access to their rich materials. Richard Jensen and Daniel Scott Smith provided a forum for me at the Newberry Library, where I presented several papers on Louisa County.

Editorial assistance has been important too. Mavis Bryant, my editor, has handled my manuscript in a highly professional manner. Carolyn Alls, Connie S. Aikens, and Lisa Donis performed miracles on my messy drafts.

I must thank the *Journal of Interdisciplinary History* editors for their permission to allow me to use material in chapter six that previously appeared in their journal, Doubleday and Company for permission to use the map of Virginia's principal geographic regions, and the Virginia State Library for the photographs in the book.

My family has contributed in ways some of which are hidden to both myself and them. My parents, Robert and Ruby Shifflett, would consider it thanks enough that I have told their story. My father did not live to see my work's completion but long enough to enjoy introducing me as "Doctor Shifflett" to all his friends. It is to his memory and to my mother that this book is dedicated. Charles Phillip and Grace White, my grandparents, have also meant much to me. Barbara, my wife, deserves more than I can or need say here. She has supported me with her teaching and made our home a cheerful place during periods of uncertainty; my affection and respect for her has grown over the years of this study. Kirsten and Zachary wanted to see their names in print.

Crandall Shifflett
Blacksburg, Virginia
15 March 1982

Patronage and Poverty
in the Tobacco South
Louisa County, Virginia, 1860–1900

·

I

•

The Social Structure
of Louisa County, Virginia, 1860–1900

Poverty in Louisa was not simply a product of the American Civil War. The history of the rural South after 1865 cannot be separated from its past of slavery and class rule, even by so great an event. In fact, a mythical Rip Van Winkle of Louisa County, Virginia, having fallen asleep in 1860, might have recognized little change upon waking in 1870. He would have found the Watson family still living at "Bracketts" and the Morris family at "Sylvania," both large estates located in the Green Springs district in northwest Louisa, the area of the most fertile and arable soil in the county; or the Winston family at "Edgewood" and the Goodwin family at "Oaksby." These families had acquired their estates during the eighteenth century, and subsequent generations of family members had enlarged and improved them. Louisa's Rip Van Winkle might have seen familiar faces in the fields, even more convincing proof of continuity than patrimonial estates. For example, a visit to the plantation of Thomas S. Watson would have found Charlie Robinson, Andrew Kinney, Peter Homes, William Mitchell, and other former slaves working at Bracketts from sunup to sundown and living in cabins they had inhabited as slaves. If this mythical figure had visited the courthouse in Louisa, he would have found business as usual being conducted by lawyers, doctors, and former slaveowning planters. Going to the shelves and opening the landbook of 1860, he might have recorded the names of all those planters with 500 acres or more of land. Checking this against the landbook of 1870, he would have found at least two out of three of those same names with farms about the same size as 1860.

If Louisa's Rip Van Winkle had been observant and persistent, he might have detected some signs of change: a destroyed bridge, fence, or barn; fewer livestock; less tobacco in the fields; more black laborers on the roads drifting in the direction of cities like Norfolk or Richmond; much talk at the country stores about the difficulty in getting "good help," or complaints about the lack of money and credit and about high taxes; and perhaps not a few remarks about what the North was trying to ram down the southern throat in the name of "Reconstruction," a term he would not have understood. An even more perceptive Rip might have noted that willbooks at the courthouse no longer passed along slaves "and their natural increase" to sons and daughters of slaveowners. He might even have noticed that the county generally seemed poorer and less prosperous than it had in 1870. However, the similarity of 1870 to 1860 would have been more striking.

In fact, Louisa's social structure, as measured by the distribution of land and personal property, was hardly affected by the Civil War. Neither was there a great turnover in landowners. Nevertheless, the war was important in other ways. What role did the Civil War play in Louisa's economic history? What was the nature and extent of change in Louisa's social structure during the entire postwar era up to 1900? Answers to these questions are essential to an understanding of the origins and development of patronage and poverty after the war.

BACKDROP

Louisa County lies in the central Virginia Piedmont. It is 16 miles wide and 30 miles long and contains 323,008 acres of mixed forest, meadow, and farm land, mostly a variety of cecil loam soils. Two major rivers course through the county: the North Anna flows in a southeasterly direction and with Negro Run constitutes the northern boundary; the South Anna flows in a southwesterly direction about four miles from the southern boundary. The county seat is Louisa, which is 80 miles southwest of Washington, D. C., and 45 miles northwest of the state capital in Richmond. The county has remained overwhelmingly rural; the town of Louisa, the largest center of population, today contains only about four hundred residents.

Traders and frontier families formed the first wave of settlement between 1700 and 1720. Over the next two decades land patents were purchased in average lots of 400 acres, and patentees moved from the nearby counties of Hanover and New Kent. Charles Chiswell was the largest patentee, purchasing 20,000 acres, which he disposed of in small parts. By 1740 the idea of a distinct county had

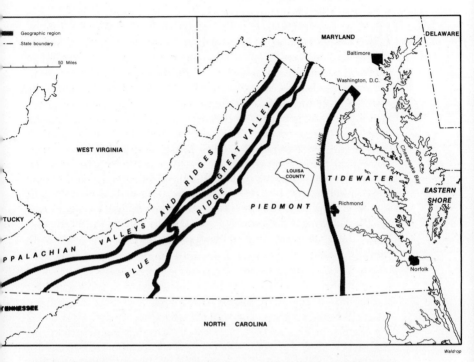

Virginia's Principal Geographic Regions Showing the Location of
Louisa County. (Prepared by Karen Waldrop using map from VIR-
GINIA: The New Dominion by Virginius Dabney. Copyright ©
1971 by Virginius Dabney. Reprinted by permission of Doubleday
& Co., Inc.)

spread; Louisa was separated from Hanover and named in honor of the daughter of George II.[1]

Early settlers chose tobacco as the basis of commercial agriculture, and it proved to be a problem staple from the very beginning. Tobacco is an exhaustive crop of both labor and soil.[2] In the early spring, seedbeds are prepared, usually by burning trash or piles of wood on patches of ground to sterilize the soil and kill any weeds. Tobacco seed lacks any reserve food, and when the seed sprouts the young plant cannot stand competition with any other plant. After the burning, the soil is worked very thoroughly, manure is mixed in, and seeds are planted, covered, and lightly tamped; fertilizer might then be scattered over the seedbed and brush or straw piled over it to protect the early sprouting plants from frost. In May or June the young plants are transplanted to hills and cultivated frequently with hoes, plows, harrows, or cultivators to keep the soil loose and free of weeds. As the plant grows, the stalk often produces suckers that have to be pruned away so that the leaves higher on the stalk will grow; the stalks must also be topped to prevent the plant from "going to seed" (flowering). The most unpleasant task is weekly worming; large green worms are removed and crushed by hand. In the fall, tobacco plants have to be cut, dried, sorted, and packed for shipment. By the final stages of harvest, it is time to prepare seedbeds for next year's crop, and the cycle repeats itself. It is such a busy staple that tobacco farmers call it "the thirteen month crop." Before the Civil War the whole process was so laborious that about two acres per slave could be grown under ideal conditions. Thus, unlike the sugar and cotton plantations where many slaves might be used efficiently at peak periods of work during the year, tobacco plantations required a small, closely supervised workforce which was kept busy most of the year just on tobacco.[3]

Tobacco is also a difficult crop because of its effects upon the soil. It can be grown on one tract of land for no longer than two to three years. By then the humus is extracted, the phosphate and potash taken away, and the topsoil turned into a fine powder easily leached by rains. A farmer might use up to 50 acres in a lifetime, the additional acreage coming from constant land clearing. Yet Virginia farmers continued to grow tobacco profitably. As the agricultural historian of the years 1815 to 1860 has concluded, "Tobacco planters were not slovenly farmers but hardheaded businessmen who knew that their methods of tillage, while destructive, were economically sound from their point of view."[4]

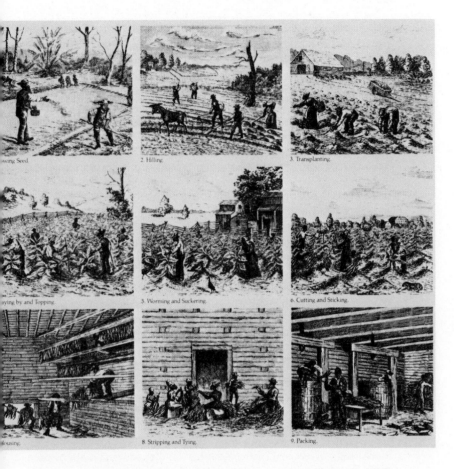

Tobacco—Hand Culture and Treatment as Recorded in 1865. (From *The Growth of Industrial Art*).

Signs of the decline in the tobacco economy of the upper South appeared early in the nineteenth century and continued up to the Civil War, as tobacco growers began to pay the high costs of years of land abuse. Declining yields and limited areas of expansion convinced some farmers that they could no longer deal with price fluctuations, as they had in the past, by increasing production. Thomas Jefferson, plagued by such troubles as an absentee proprietor, bad management of slaves, poor packing of tobacco, difficulties in getting the crop to market, and frost damage, abandoned tobacco in adjoining Albermarle County; James Madison and James Monroe experienced similar problems in the same county. Other tobacco planters of Virginia invested in sugar and cotton lands in Arkansas, Mississippi, and Louisiana, relocating with their slaves to these areas. In 1840 Virginia had 20,670 fewer slaves than in 1830.[5] In Louisa County, the white population declined by almost 2 percent and the slave population by 4 percent during the 1830s.[6]

Slaveholding planters responded in more positive ways to soil exhaustion and sought to restore profits through crop rotation and diversification, contour and deep plowing, and the application of lime, guano, marl, and plaster, or the planting of clover as a cover crop. These efforts increased in the two decades before the Civil War, and tobacco production rose by 54 percent in Virginia and Maryland. Corn yields also increased by 10 percent, and farmers paid more attention to wheat as a cash crop; grass farming and dairying rose as well.[7]

Louisa's slaveholders diversified too, as the last census of agriculture taken before the Civil War revealed. Charles Dickenson's farm produced 9,000 pounds of tobacco in 1860, but he also harvested 750 bushels of wheat, 1,000 bushels of corn, 310 bushels of oats, and small amounts of potatoes, butter, and honey to satisfy household needs. Dickenson had ten milking cows and Thomas S. Watson seven, and both raised cattle and hogs. Dickenson also had eighteen sheep which produced 60 pounds of wool in 1860. The demand for dairy and poultry produce from the nearby urban centers of Richmond and Washington, D. C., was not yet strong enough to encourage expansion in these areas of farming, however.

In spite of what has been argued, diversification and scientific agricultural practices did not halt out-migration in Virginia or lead to widespread land redistribution.[8] In the Old Dominion, twenty-four counties lost population in the 1850s. Louisa County's white population dropped by 4 percent while the slave population showed only a 3 percent increase.[9] Moreover, Virginia still had more farms of 500 or more acres than any state in the South, except Georgia, the average size being 324 acres, hardly evidence of the advance of the small farmer.[10]

In spite of these signs of agricultural decline in the upper South counties, slaves in Virginia and Louisa remained important numerically and therefore continued to be great sources of wealth and income, as records of the federal census and the tax and willbooks of Louisa County showed. According to the 1860 census, Virginia led the South in both the number of slaves and slaveholders, surpassing Georgia, its closest rival, by about 11,000 slaveholders and 28,000 slaves. In Louisa County nearly two out of every three white families owned at least one slave, compared with the South in general, where slaveholders constituted about one-fourth of all families. About 62 percent of the county's population in 1860 was slave. Louisa's slaveholders also owned larger numbers of slaves than the regional average. About 45 percent owned more than nineteen slaves, while the same was true of only 28 percent of southern planters overall.[11]

In 1863, when tax revenue on slaves peaked in Louisa, the county collected $58,389 or about 57 percent of its total income, from this form of taxation.[12] Important to the county in terms of the revenue they generated, slaves also constituted a major portion of the assets of individual landowners. It was not unusual for them to compose one-half or more of a planter's total estate. Such was the case with Charles Dickenson, whose total estate was appraised at $22,000 in 1859: $11,000 in slaves (twelve adults, two of whom the appraisers considered of no economic value, and six children), $4,900 in land (545 acres), and $6,100 in other kinds of personal property; or Nelson Moss, whose slaves (twenty-five of various ages and six small children) sold for about $31,000 in 1859 while his land (516 acres) went for $6,700; or the wealthy William Morris, who amassed an estate worth $114,000: $45,000 in slaves, $27,700 in land (1,200 acres), $18,500 in stock certificates of railroads, banks, and an insurance company, $14,300 in private bonds, and the remaining $7,600 in crops, livestock, and other personal property. Depending upon age and health, slave values in Louisa ranged from $800 each for young boys and girls to $1,450 for healthy male or female youths in 1859. Values began to decline about age thirty-five, dropping to their lowest points in old age.[13] Even the small slaveholder of one to ten slaves, a holding representative of the majority of Louisa and southern slaveholders, might have held an asset valued at $14,500 if he held ten healthy young men and women.[14]

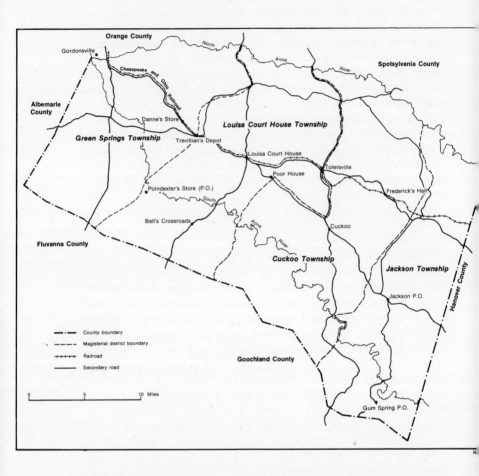

Louisa County, Virginia, c. 1871. (Prepared by Karen Waldrop from
an 1871 geological survey map of Louisa County. Courtesy: Library
of Congress.

Thus, on the eve of the Civil War, Louisa represented the economically shaky tobacco counties of the upper South that were attempting to adjust to the problem of soil exhaustion and the threat this posed to planter income. Yet planters had no intention of abandoning slavery. In fact, slaves continued to be the primary source of planter wealth and county revenue, and the Louisa economy remained firmly wedded to the plantation system of agricultural production. The slaveholding families' accumulation of generations had created a cushion against market vicissitudes in the form of chattel property; human beings grew like horses, cattle, or tobacco plants and were more elastic assets than any of these. Slaves could be accumulated, rented, worked, loaned, willed, taxed, used as collateral to secure loans, traded, or sold. No other property was so flexible—or so valuable.

LOUISA'S AGRICULTURAL DECLINE, 1860–1900

Between 1860 and the twentieth century, economic hardship and widespread poverty cursed man and land in Louisa County. It was a period of war; declining farm prices; reduced farm, machinery, and livestock values; high death rates; heavy out-migration; marginal household budgets; and general scarcity and want. Subsequent chapters will deal with all of these developments. However, a general picture of Louisa's economic trends can be gained by a comparison of the county with other parts of the United States during the same period.

A picture of the decline of agriculture in Louisa and the cotton South is available in Table 1.1, which compares Louisa with the cotton-growing county of Greene, Georgia, and two fast-growing frontier counties of the Midwest.[15] Most striking are the retrogressive trends of the South, contrasting sharply with the progressive agriculture of the frontier West. As Table 1.1 indicates, per capita improved acreage in Louisa dropped by 27 percent between 1860 and 1900 while Hamilton County, Iowa, increased the acreage under cultivation by two and one-half times per person. Great increases in machinery and livestock in Hamilton and Trempealeau allowed these counties to expand the acreage under cultivation. Finally, per capita farm values dropped in all these counties, reflecting the malaise in agriculture generally, but the drop was more stunning in the southern counties.

Table 1.1   Changes in Population and Per Capita
Agricultural Holdings, Louisa and Selected Counties,
1860–1900

	Population (percent change)	Improved Acres (percent change)	Farms (value in dollars)	Machinery (value in dollars)	Livestock (value in dollars)
Louisa (Va.)	−1	−27	−91	−8	−29
Greene (Ga.)	+30	−41	−89	−37	−52
Hamilton (Ia.)	+1048	+247	−26	+40	+343
Trempealeau (Wis.)	+802	+144	−47	+25	+154

Source: Compiled from the following U.S. censuses: *Eighth Census, 1860: Agriculture,* 22–23, 46–47, 154–67; *Twelfth Census, 1900: Population,* vol. I, pt. 1, pp. 18–19, 46–47, 624–26, 639; *Twelfth Census, 1900: Agriculture,* vol. V, pt. 1, pp. 271, 276, 302–6, 426–27, 487–90.

Starting as mere outposts on America's frontier in 1860, Hamilton County, Iowa, and Trempealeau County, Wisconsin, surpassed in just over a generation what the two southern counties had taken centuries to accumulate. Immigrants, especially Germans and Scandinavians, fueled much of the growth in midwestern counties, but a significant number of settlers, particularly in the 1850s, were sons of Kentucky, Tennessee, and Virginia farmers in flight from the kinds of economic malaise reflected in this table.[16] There they found easier credit, more fertile soil, and a land more agreeable to exploitation by farm machinery. While the amount of improved acreage in the southern counties decreased, the accumulation of yield-producing factors (horses and machinery) in counties like Trempealeau permitted the bringing of some 240,000 additional acres under the plow.[17] It is not hard to understand the magnetic appeal this area held for southerners and other settlers.

Horsepower was fundamental to agricultural progress. Oxen had certain advantages over horses: they usually weighed more, were more powerful in the yoke, and often more tractable; they consumed less food, could withstand more heat, and were cheaper. However, they had definite disadvantages: they were slower, more clumsy, and less well-heeled than the farm horse.[18] Technological developments in farm machinery after the 1830s made the ox less desirable because the new machinery demanded a sure-footed, nimble, and fast draft animal like the horse, if the farmer was to take advantage of opportunities for increasing production. Oxen were of little value with steel and iron plows, disc harrows, grain drills, planters, reapers, straddle-row cultivators and rakes, machinery already in use in the north-central states by 1870.[19] In Illinois, for example, the ox hung on longest in the southern portion of the state, where the mechanization of agriculture proceeded more slowly. Even before the Civil War, however, "The day of the ox was passing."[20]

When the use of oxen is taken as a measure of mechanization and Louisa is compared with the midwestern counties of Hamilton and Trempealeau on this basis, it is obvious that mechanization in Louisa lagged far behind that of the frontier counties. In 1880, 38 percent of Louisa's draft power was still being supplied by working oxen, compared with 0.2 percent and 10 percent in Hamilton and Trempealeau, respectively.[21] Among a sample of those who listed their occupation as "farmer" on the 1880 manuscript census of population, just over one-half of the white sample population owned oxen.[22] About 76 percent of white sample farmers farmed with horses too, but only 28 percent of the black sample owned horses. Contrary to conventional wisdom about the place of mules in the South, 96 percent of the black sample and about three-fourths of the white sample used no mules in 1880! The day of the ox had not passed in Louisa, according to the last agricultural census prior to the twentieth century. In the South in general, the value of farm equipment in 1900 was less than a half of the 1860 value, and, since valuation in the rest of the country had doubled, the reduction reflects not merely the effects of agricultural depression, but a genuine lag in mechanization.[23]

With great advantages in horsepower,[24] farmers of the Corn Belt were able to surmount the agricultural depression of the period between 1866 and 1896, years when the prices of agricultural commodities fell, as did prices in general, and to build "one of the most prosperous agricultural economies the world had ever seen in this land.[25] As land values in Louisa dropped to as low as $2.00 per acre by the close of the century, land in central Illinois and eastern Iowa, which had been purchased at $1.25 per acre in the 1830s and 1840s, commanded prices of $40 to $60 per acre and higher.[26] In 1880, even the lowly agricultural ranks of tenant and sharecropper in Trempealeau County had median holdings of 133 and 163 acres, respectively, and the median value of their livestock ($268 for tenants and $400 for sharecroppers) would have placed them comfortably within the ranks of Louisa's largeholding class.[27] The historian of Trempealeau concluded, not without understatement, "It is obvious that tenants in Trempealeau were nothing like the sharecroppers in the South."[28]

Historians have credited the decline or stagnation of the southern economy after 1865 to the destructive effects of the Civil War. However, Louisa's decline had not begun with the war. As noted above, soil depletion and fluctuations in tobacco prices prompted some tobacco farmers to migrate to the South and West as early as the 1830s and others to shift to other forms of farming decades before the war.

THE ROLE OF THE CIVIL WAR

Louisa County played a substantial military role in the Civil War. It sent seven companies to the front, a total of about one thousand native sons.[29] It was the site of one of the largest all cavalry battles of the war at Trevillians Depot, just five miles west of the courthouse. Confederate generals Wade Hampton and Fitzhugh Lee with 5,000 soldiers faced Union generals Phil Sheridan and George Custer with 8,000 soldiers and in two days of heavy fighting the Confederates won, killing 102 Union soldiers, wounding 470, and taking 570 prisoners. Union forces killed 59 Confederates, wounded 258, and took 435 prisoners.[30]

Contemporary accounts of damage to property and livestock are scattered but suggestive of the kinds of losses. Northern raiders visited the county several times. The most destructive raids were those of General Stoneman's cavalry in May 1863 and General Dahlgren's cavalry in February 1864. In both cases, observers reported damage to homes, mills, bridges, fences, and the railway. However, the greatest losses were in livestock and foodstores. About 220 horses and mules were killed at Thompson's Crossroads and an equal number at Yancyville in southern and eastern Louisa. Persons living in the vicinity of Thompson's Crossroads were reported to have "lost everything; all the corn, bacon, fowls, flour, hogs, etc." Another resident reported, "We have been visited three times by Northern raiders . . . they left us no corn, meat, oats or fodder. They left us without food. They killed nearly all of my hogs and some of the cattle and sheep . . . ."[31]

An idea of the overall impact of the war in the county may be gained by comparing the personal property taxbooks before and after the conflict. Horses, cattle, sheep, hogs, farm implements, kitchen and household furniture, clocks and watches, pianos, sewing machines, carriages, and investments in bonds and mining and manufacturing enterprises constituted the taxable personal property of Louisa, and together with land, assessments on this property were the sources of the county's revenue. Between 1863 and 1866 Louisa tax records show reductions of nearly one-third in the numbers of sheep and hogs, one-fourth in cattle, and almost one-fifth in horses (Table 1.2). These losses had far-reaching consequences, as they affected sources of food, draft power, and tax revenue.[32]

Table 1.2   Numbers of Livestock, Louisa County,
1863 and 1866

Kind	1863	1866	*Percent Reduced*
Horses	3,044	2,473	−18
Cattle	7,934	6,146	−22
Sheep	7,360	5,048	−31
Hogs	13,825	9,528	−31

Source: Personal Property Taxbook, Louisa County, 1863 and 1866.

The war brought budgetary anemia to Louisa as the great wealth generated by counting people as property gave way to the financial realities of legally free labor. As noted above, taxes on slaves had filled county coffers in 1863 with $58,389 in revenue, a figure which constituted about two-thirds of all personal property tax income for that year.[33] By 1870, however, this munificent source of income had evaporated, and Louisa collected a mere $7,046 on the remaining taxable personal property. Draft animals and livestock, bedsteads and dressers, gold watches and pianos, hoes and scythes, bonds and notes, grist mills and quartz mines, none of these alone nor all of them together produced the lavish sums the county had once collected on human flesh. Even when combined with land tax revenues of about $18,000, Louisa's total tax income for 1870 was only one-fourth of that for 1863.[34]

To summarize the impact of the Civil War, Louisa County lost as much as one-third of its livestock and three-fourths of its tax base. Individual planters saw the value of their estates halved by the elimination of slaves as chattel property; a dependable and ever-expanding source of money for roads, bridges, public buildings, administrative salaries and expenses, and the general welfare was "gone with the wind." These were severe assaults upon Louisa's economy, and those who lived through these difficult times may have been exaggerating only slightly when they claimed they "lost everything." However, contemporary observers did exaggerate the meaning of the war for the social structure; many felt that the old order was gone with the wind, too. In that case, their imaginations served them too well. In Louisa, the Civil War was destructive but it proved to be no watershed for the plantation economy, as an examination of the social structure between 1860 and 1900 will show.

STRUCTURAL CHANGE, 1860–1900

After the Civil War many southerners went to extremes to lure northern investment capital into the region. Often their efforts took the form of boosterism; the South was touted as a land on the move from agricultural backwardness to a modern industrial state. In brief, a "New South" was in the making. These prophets of progress borrowed from many sources and traditions. Gradually, their argument evolved into one combining fact and fiction. Ultimately, it lead to a denial of the region's most salient features of poverty and racism.[35] An important part of the Big Lie about the New South assigned to the Civil War the role of economic watershed. Allegedly, it had not only freed the slaves but emancipated poor whites, who were now on the rise—"on the rise" presumably because the large plantations were breaking up, at least according to federal census records of the late nineteenth century. In 1905, the work of Enoch Marvin Banks indicated that the census had exaggerated the celebrated breakup, certainly in Georgia. In 1902, 4 percent of Georgia landowners held one-quarter of the land.[36] A more direct challenge to the myth came in 1937 in the work of Roger W. Shugg in Louisiana. Using county tax records, he found that the plantation not only had survived, but actully expanded, in the postwar period.[37] Later, in 1951, C. Vann Woodward found further proof of the plantation's survival. More striking, however, was Woodward's argument that the plantation class itself, if not the plantation, had in a sense broken up. According to this view, a new class of industrial capitalists had seized power from the planter class.[38] More recently, Jonathan M. Wiener has challenged the belief in the breakup of the planter class by using data from Marengo County in Alabama's cotton belt.[39] It is at the county level where these generalizations can best be tested.

In Louisa, the war dissolved a major source of income and reduced the wealth of large estates, but it figured little in changing the number of owners or the size of holdings. In this regard, Louisa resembled the rest of the South. Table 1.3 shows that between 1860 and 1870, the total number of owners in Louisa increased by 16 percent, an average increase of less than 2 percent a year between 1860 and 1870.[40] Moreover, large estates, with great investments in land and slaves where spectacular changes might have been expected as a result of the war, showed only a 4 percent decrease in the 1860s. Although these changes suggest future trends, they indicate that the war itself did not destroy the plantation farm.

Table 1.3 Number of Owners and Landholdings by Size, Louisa County, 1860 and 1870

	1860	*1870*	*Percent Change*
Total owners	1,160	1,357	+16
1–100 acre holdings	383	519	+35
101–300 acre holdings	409	488	+19
301+ acre holdings	368	350	−4

Source: Land Taxbook, Louisa County, 1860 and 1870.

Furthermore, in spite of what has been argued, the war did not disrupt planters, either. In Louisa, at least, there was no "revolution in land titles," no replacement of an old aristocracy by a new, more adventurous, and speculative aristocracy, as was the case among the sugar and cotton plantations of the deep South.[41] Instead, county landbooks reflect striking continuity in traditional land ownership patterns. Of the 145 owners in 1860 who held 500 acres or more, from two-thirds to three-fourths showed up in a search of county landbooks in 1870 with holdings almost the same size.[42] The positive location in the county of at least two of every three formerly large slaveholders after ten years of war and uncertainty is strong evidence of continuity in patterns of landholding. A similar persistence has been found in the cotton South in Marengo County, Alabama.[43]

Neither do Louisa landbooks which recorded the residence of the landowner support the influx of "outsiders," which were apparently common elsewhere in the South. Of the 61 nonresident landowners in 1870, all but 15 percent lived in adjoining counties or cities. By 1900 the percentage had reached 35, yet total nonresident owners still constituted only 4 percent of all owners.[44]

If the war did not accomplish the celebrated breakup of the plantation or dislodge former planters, a striking growth in the number of owners, especially those holding under 100 acres, marked the period between 1870 and 1900, as Table 1.4 reveals. As the total number of owners grew by two and one-half times, the number of smallholders increased more than fourfold while the number of those holding over 300 acres diminished by more than one-third. Some increase in the number of landowners might have been anticipated merely as a result of population growth, but this was not the case. In fact, out-migration siphoned off much of this growth, and the federal census counted 174 fewer people in Louisa in 1900 than in 1870.[45] Table 1.4 also documents a remarkable rise in the number of black owners, who jumped from only 22 in 1870 to 1,314 in 1900, composing 39 percent of all owners by the latter date.[46] Blacks still owned only 11 percent of the land while making up 52 percent of the population,[47] but what seems more significant is the unexpected progress of destitute former slaves who had somehow acquired tiny plots of their own land. It was impossible to identify the origins of all these landowners precisely, but among the "farmer" sample population, where name tracing was possible, less than 1 percent were landowners in 1870 compared with 35 percent in 1900, according to landbooks of those years. Thus, substantial numbers of black Louisans had become landholders.

Such a striking growth in the number of landowners would seem to be proof of egalitarianism on the march, a trend sure to produce fundamental changes in the county's social structure. Not only had the total number of owners grown, but as a percentage of the entire population they had increased by three times between 1860 and 1900. Table 1.5, which examines the top 5 percent of landed wealth in Louisa County before and after the war, appears also to support an argument for growing equality. When the average percentage of land held in the period by *each* of the wealthiest landholders in the top 5 percent in the county was calculated, for example, it became

apparent that the economic influence of large *individual* holders had
been reduced by one-half (from .0038 to .0018).[48]

Table 1.4   Number of Owners and Landholdings by Size,
Louisa County, 1870 and 1900

	1870	1900	Percent Change
Total owners	1,357	3,337	+146
1–100 acre holdings	519	2,353	+353
101–300 acre holdings	488	767	+57
301 + acre holdings	350	217	−38
Black owners	22	1,314	+5,873

Source: Land Taxbook, Louisa County, 1870 and 1900.

Table 1.5   Top 5 Percent of Landholders, Louisa County,
1860 and 1900

	1860	1900
Number of landholders	58	167
Percentage of county's land held by group	22	30
Average percentage held by individuals	.0038	.0018

Source: Land Taxbook, Louisa County, 1860 and 1900.

The situation, however, turned out to be even more complex. If
the county land area is conceived as a pie, the top 5 percent of the
owners had a larger slice in 1900 than 1860. In 1860, 58 farmers
owned 22 percent of the total land mass, or 69,598 acres. In 1900,
however, 167 farmers owned 30 percent of Louisa's acreage, or
93,645 acres, and 3,170 divided the remaining 70 percent. In spite
of the entry of more laborers, tenants, and sharecroppers into the
ranks of the landed, the wealthiest landowners had enlarged their
collective holdings of the total land area by 50 percent.[49]

The paradox of the accompaniment of tenants' mobility with
growing inequality may seem more explicable with a reexamination
of the changes in land tenure reflected in Table 1.4, where it is
obvious that most of those entering the ranks of the landed were

smallholders who were acquiring tiny portions of the vast acreages of the largeholders. In 1880, for example, the "farmer" sample also reveals that, in spite of a growing number of owners, a great gap opened between black freeholders and their white counterparts. The mean freeholding size among freedmen was 24 acres while the whites' meanholding was 299 acres.[50] Thus, in Louisa, land transfer was not necessarily a pathway to greater equality; rather, it proceeded in the midst of a growing concentration of landed wealth.

However, land was only part of the story. Too much has been made of this resource alone as a measure of wealth and mobility. As settlers pushed westward in the nineteenth century, some soon discovered land to be the fool's gold of agriculture.[51] After the Civil War, former slaves thirsted for land as the ultimate symbol and substance of freedom and independence, only to be disappointed by how little its possession actually changed their status. Historians too have often stressed land to the exclusion of other productive factors of agriculture.[52] Except for the speculator, land by itself cannot produce income.

It is remarkable how little attention has been paid to the income-generating factors of agricultural production besides land.[53] Horses, mules, oxen, cattle, hoes, plows, harrows, and other implements are also yield- or income-producing factors of agriculture. The ownership of these factors figured heavily in the distribution of wealth, and command over these resources in addition to land largely determined the standard of living for the farmers of Louisa.[54] More significantly, the economic and social mobility of each Louisa farmer rested upon his holdings of these productive factors. Several examples drawn from Louisa records and the federal censuses underscore the relationship between all these factors of production and economic success.[55]

Edward P. Boxley was born in Virginia in 1843 and by 1880 had settled in Louisa County with Mary, his thirty-five-year-old wife, two sons: Clarence, age thirteen, and Frank, age twelve, and two daughters: Nannie, age nine, and Ida, age four. In 1880 Edward rented on shares a farm which totaled 470 acres and was valued at $5,000–$6,000. About 200 acres were "improved," and in 1880 he planted 18 percent of the improved acreage in corn, 13 percent in wheat, 10 percent in oats, and he fallowed the rest. His machinery was valued at $76–$100 and livestock at $201–$300, which included twenty-three chickens, nine pigs, four milch cows, and one beef cow. In the fields, he used two horses and a pair of oxen. During the year he even managed to hire the monetary equivalent of one laborer full time ($101–$200), and his products were valued at about $750 for the year. Boxley did so well that by 1890 he was able to purchase 61 acres valued at $8 per acre, and the 1900 federal census indicated that this fifty-seven-year-old former sharecropper owned his farm free and clear, including his house. In personal property, county records reflected the worth of his draft animals and livestock to be the same in 1900 as 1880, his machinery depreciated to no value, and his furniture doubled to a value of about $65.

William Mitchell was born into slavery in Louisa in 1830 and grew up on the plantation of Thomas Watson. After the war he continued on Watson's farm as one of his tenants. The 1870 census revealed that Mitchell, now married and trying to raise a family of six children, held no real estate or personal property of value. County records, however, showed him owning a milch cow and pigs worth $11–$25 and furniture worth about $5. He owned no draft animals or machinery. By 1880 Mitchell's family consisted of Louisa, his forty-three-year-old wife; Eliza, his nineteen-year-old daughter now separated from her husband; Fannie, his twenty-two-year-old daughter who worked as a maid; daughters Susan, age fourteen, Lainene, age thirteen, and Maggie, age three; sons Fontane, age eighteen, and Tommie, age seventeen, both of whom worked as farmhands; and sons William, age nine, and Joseph, age six. Mary, his grandchild (Eliza's daughter), also lived in the household. In 1880 Mitchell farmed 5 acres, on which he grew a little pulse and nothing else. In that same year, he bought 7 acres of land jointly with Lewis Ragland which local landbooks assessed at $40 an acre! Buildings on the property were assessed at $200. In 1900, this seventy-year-old former slave still owned his 7 acres, valued at $14 per acre, with buildings assessed at $56. However, he was destitute of any other personal property, indeed poorer than he had been in 1880.

These two examples highlight the importance of either owning or gaining access to factors of production. Boxley already owned or could use draft animals, machinery, and livestock before he became a landowner. In fact, these assets greatly enhanced his mobility and enabled him to buy land. Mitchell, on the other hand, became a landowner partially through the contributions of his employed sons and by liquidating what few additional assets he had, and even then it was not all his. In his case, as with so many other small landowners, land ownership had not freed him from tenantry , made him economically independent or insulated him from poverty. It proved impossible to determine the number of petty landowners who also worked as tenants or for hire. Given their poverty, however, it must have been a large number.

These case histories suggest another potentially important difference: Boxley was white. Boxley rented an obviously valuable farm with ample machinery and draft power, which eased his path to land ownership. Mitchell managed to rent a very small plot but lacked access to any other income-generating factors. When they did become landowners, Boxley's land was assessed at $8 and Mitchell's at $40 per acre. Of course, examples of white tenants with histories similar to Mitchell's could also be found. Mordecai Shiflet, for example, was a poor white farmer before the Civil War; in 1870 this eighty-two-year-old tenant farmer of 20 acres owned no horses, mules, oxen, or machinery. He lived by growing a little corn to feed his one milch cow and pigs and selling an occasional calf. However, the number of whites in such circumstances was always smaller than the number of blacks, and even in this case evidence of preferential tax treatment surfaced. Shiflet paid no taxes in 1870 on livestock which the census found him owning. The racial roots of poverty will be explored in greater detail later.

Table 1.6   Top 5 Percent of Personal Property Holders, Louisa County, 1863 and 1900

	1863	1900
Number of property holders	110	139
Percentage of county's personal property held by group	32	56
Average percentage held by individuals	.0048	.0036

Source: Personal Property Taxbook, Louisa County, 1863 and 1900.

Note: As in the case of Table 1.5, above, perfect equality would have found the top 5 percent owning 5 percent of all personal property and each person among the top 5 percent with an equal share of property. In actual figures, the top 5 percent owned $2,628,055 worth of taxable personal property in 1863 and $282,082 in 1900.

The same records which provided the information for these case histories may also be used to gauge the overall patterns in personal property holdings between the war and the twentieth century. Table 1.6 was derived from the taxbooks of 1863 and 1900.[56] Just as in the case of land, the holdings of personal property followed the same patterns of dispersion and concentration, except that inequality was even greater in this vital area. Table 1.6 shows that while the average percentage of wealth held by each of the top 5 percent declined between 1863 and 1900, holdings of livestock, draft animals, and farm implements (and furniture) became 75 percent more concentrated. By 1900 the top 5 percent held 56 percent of the county's taxable personal property, whereas in 1863 they had controlled about one-third. Put another way, in 1900, 95 percent of all males twenty-one years of age and older divided among themselves less than half the county's livestock, draft animals, furniture, and machinery. Yet, the individual shares of each member of the top 5 percent were smaller (.0048 to .0036). Thus, wealth was more evenly distributed in 1900 than in 1863, but among the wealthy only.

THE SOCIAL STRUCTURE AND CLASS RULE

Louisa's class structure survived the Civil War intact, a fact of great importance in Louisa's postwar history. Planters lost livestock and suffered damages to crops, buildings, and horses, but they could recover these losses as long as they were not dispossessed of their wealth and advantages in land, tools, livestock, and other assets. The war did not, therefore, destroy the economic hegemony of the planter class, in spite of the impressive growth of black landowners.

Indeed, this study of Louisa illustrates how the rise of "petty proprietorship" guaranteed economic stagnation for Louisa and poverty for owners of tiny plots.[57] Why? Louisa was tied historically to a "surplus-extraction" structure, i.e., slavery, whereby the ruling class siphoned off the surplus of direct producers. After the war, the surplus continued to be extracted because the war failed to derail the surplus-extraction structure. The growth of petty holdings played into the hands of the ruling class—it provided another means of extraction whereby planters sold off small portions of their estates for liquid capital, and land acquisition exhausted the assets of petty holders, leaving them land-poor. More importantly, the income-generating factors of agriculture were even more concentrated than land, which immobilized petty holders and the landless and perpetuated the surplus-extraction structure.

If the Civil War was not an economic revolution, it promised to become one. The elimination of slave labor posed a serious challenge to the planter class, especially their capacity to extract a surplus. The source of the continuity in class rule, in spite of the destruction of the slave labor system, is the subject of the next chapter, which examines the social structure as a set of dynamic relationships between employers and employees. A system of patronage developed into the handmaid of poverty.

II

·

Patrons and Clients:
From Paternalism to Patronage

When the slave labor system of the South collapsed with the Civil War, paternalism, which had been the basis of the master-slave relationship, expired with it, according to a recent study of slavery.[1] In Louisa, paternalism was replaced by a system of patronage.[2] In its practical operation, it divided Louisans into two groups—patrons and clients. Patrons were those who monopolized the income-generating factors of agriculture, not just land, but draft animals, livestock, tools, and credit. Clients were those who bargained with patrons for employment, housing, loans, rent, and general access to means of production. As an economic system, patronage was capitalism in another form. In political terms, it developed into a kind of government. In social relations, the term might be used to stand for the countless acts of deference the economically and politically powerless paid the custodians of power. This chapter describes patronage as an economic system. It shows how federal and state laws encouraged the growth of patronage capitalism. At the local level, labor contracts and lien agreements crystallized patronage into a fixed hierarchy of work relationships. A close examination of these relationships illuminates the functional role of patronage as a surplus-extraction structure.

I have already elaborated patronage as an economic system.[3] To summarize, it was a form of capitalism whereby the means of production and distribution were privately owned and operated for profit, as is customary in capitalist economies, but where no fully competitive market in labor functioned. Moreover, the position of labor also set it apart from slave capitalism, which it replaced, and free-labor capitalism such as existed in the North. Labor was no longer legally bound as property to an employer, but it was economically enslaved. European peasants had far more freedom and independence than postwar southern laborers. German and Scandinavian immigrants to the Midwest, though poor, often had their own tools, livestock, sources of credit, or cash reserves, independent of their employer-landlord, and they were free to homestead. Neither did northern labor face an historical tradition of labor repression justified in racial terms. Patronage capitalism was a product both of this historical tradition and the mutual needs of capital and labor in the Emancipation Period.

In spite of tradition and postwar economic exigencies, the institutional support of government at various levels was crucial to the development of patronage capitalism in Louisa. As the Civil War drew to a close, the Union government turned its attention from the battlefields to the massive problem of southern labor and its new relationship to capital.

UNION POLICY AND PATRONAGE

The Union government refused to guarantee or even allow a freely competitive market in labor during the Reconstruction period. Through the enactment of various laws and codes dealing with labor and employer-employee relationships, Reconstruction leaders impeded the free movement of labor and encouraged former slaves to sign labor contracts with their former masters. Beyond helping to secure labor contracts and providing small rations of food and clothing, federal and state officials offered freedmen no economic assistance. The belief was that the neutral laws of the market economy would eventually mitigate inequalities as freedmen advanced; to go further would constitute tampering with the natural operation of these laws. Yet, the Union government did not feel it was interfering with the free market when it set restrictions on labor's mobility and bargaining power. Given conditions of inequality, restrictions on the movement of labor, the desperate dependency of clients upon local patrons, and the drive of patrons to bind labor to its fields, patronage as a system of class domination and control had fertile soil.

Soon after the war the Union government became involved in capital-labor arrangements in the South and established guidelines which were to have far-reaching consequences for counties like Louisa. In March 1865, the Bureau of Refugees, Freedmen, and Abandoned Lands, commonly called the Freedmen's Bureau, a branch of the War Department, was established to care for refugees and supervise the transition from slave to free labor. Between June and December 1865 it issued a series of orders dealing with capital-labor arrangements. A general order in June, issued by the Richmond office of the bureau, the administrative headquarters of the Fourth District in which Louisa County was located, stated clearly that the abolition of slavery did not mean that vagrancy would be tolerated. "Neither blacks nor whites," it continued, "will be allowed to abandon their *proper* occupations, to desert their families or roam in idleness about this Department."[4]

In July the bureau issued Circular Number 11, signed by General O. O. Howard, who headed the agency; it was the federal government's solution to the general absence of cash in the postwar South. It instructed field officers throughout the South to determine in their own minds "proper" wage rates, but they were forbidden from setting a fixed rate. In addition, Circular 11 ordered that wages "be secured by a lien on the crops or land," with all agreements to be subject to the approval of the nearest agent and filed in the Washington office of the bureau. It forbade holding debtors in servitude to labor, commonly called peonage, "without proper consent."[5] In September, as reports of refusals of freedmen to enter into agreements with their former masters continued to reach Washington, field officers were told to stress that labor contracts differed from slavery; they were the mark of free laborers everywhere.[6]

Basically, the bureau wanted to get freedmen off government relief rolls, even if this meant forcing them back on their former masters. Their intention, first stated in the June general order outlined above, was underscored in a November circular, where it was explained that the role of the bureau was not to act as a conduit of government aid or private charity. Instead, it wanted freedmen to become "a self-supporting class of free laborers who shall understand the necessity of steady employment and the responsibility of providing for themselves and families." The level of Union parsimony was revealed by the Louisa field officer of the bureau in 1866 who reported that only 600 to 700 rations were issued in July to the old, destitute, helpless, and children. He estimated 5,000–7,000 freedmen to be in need.[7] The stick took precedence over the carrot, for the bureau recommended that laborers who refused employment when it was offered should be treated as vagrants.[8]

Obviously, the bureau was not sponsoring a social revolution. That much it had already made clear in its reconstruction policies in Davis Bend, Mississippi, and the Sea Islands of South Carolina, where it failed to carry through on its promises to distribute abandoned lands to freedmen.[9] "Steady employment" and "proper occupations" were key phrases in these later pronouncements, which

signaled a continuation of a more restrained policy of getting freedmen back to work. In spite of southern criticism that the bureau
encouraged freedmen to press for their civil rights, political equality,
and land, Union policy in many ways assured the continuity of
plantation agriculture. Some officials allied themselves with southern landowners and in Mississippi even cooperated with them to
force blacks to remain on plantations.[10]

Federal policy toward liberated slaves emanated, at times, from
the best of intentions. In the area of civil rights, for example, the
bureau tried to extend legal protection to former slaves, to define
and safeguard the rights of freedmen before the law. Freedmen's
Bureau Courts were established to assure fair treatment of blacks in
the courts, especially where plaintiffs were white. Freedmen also
had recourse in the courts if their employers failed to live up to their
contractual promises.

The bureau failed, however, to appreciate the frailty of civil rights
under conditions of poverty. Even during Reconstruction, when the
bureau gave legal assistance without charge, the rights of freedmen
could not be guaranteed against economic intimidation, and after the
Reconstruction era ended, redress through the courts was a luxury
freedmen could not afford.

VIRGINIA AND THE PATRONAGE SYSTEM

Legislation at the state level reinforced Union labor policy and
promoted the institutionalization of the patronage system. The
Virginia General Assembly of 1865–66 carefully defined vagrancy
as a crime and established judicial procedures for dealing with it. The
Vagrancy Act referred to a "great increase of idle and disorderly
persons" and the need for laws to deal with what might be called "the
crisis of paternalism."[11] Fearing the state would be "overrun with
dissolute and abandoned characters,"[12] the act made the following
persons liable: (1) any person who returned to any county from
which he had been legally moved; (2) all who were unable to
maintain themselves and their families and who were unemployed
and living in idleness or refused to work "for the usual and common
wages given to other laborers in the like work in the place where
they are"; (3) all who refused to perform work alloted them by the
overseer of the poor; (4) beggars; (5) all who came from outside the
state and were found loitering and residing in Virginia with no trade,

occupation, or visible means of subsistence and could give no account of themselves.[13]

Any local resident might bring a person suspected of vagrancy before a justice of the peace, who, upon finding him guilty, could order the vagrant to be employed in labor for up to three months "for the best wages available." If vagrants attempted to run away from these harsh penalties, they might be returned to the hirer and sentenced to work without pay for an additional month. The justice of the peace could also authorize employers to work laborers with a ball and chain, and if hirers refused to take runaways again, they could be assigned to the county workhouse or placed in jail to be fed on bread and water.[14] Thus was peonage instituted, and it could snare workers in flight from wage rates or working conditions, regardless of how unfair or cruel those conditions might be.

Concerns in Virginia about labor unrest provoked several other important legislative acts which fastened the grip of employers over their laborers. In 1866 the General Assembly prescribed fines for anyone enticing laborers under contract from the service of employers, and in the same year all labor contracts made between 1861 and 1865 were declared valid.[15] A penalty of five to ten years in prison was instituted for conspiracy to incite one race against the other,[16] and searches and seizures of "public" arms were authorized and carried out.[17] In Louisa County, one conscientious patrol seized not only government arms (i.e., guns from the Civil War), but all arms found in a search of freedmen's houses at Christmas of 1865.[18] Confiscation of firearms was a serious threat to freedmen, not merely to their future safety or their ability to take up arms against oppressors, an unlikely possibility anyhow, but to their health. Without guns, the Louisa poor could not supplement their meager diets by hunting.

Thus, federal and state governments during Reconstruction produced a "net of laws" to guarantee labor and limit its mobility. Indeed, the South's labor system differed from the "classically capitalist North" because of just such a "web of restrictive legislation." Northern farm laborers were free to move around and negotiate for the best terms of employment, but a similar effort by southern labor lead to fines, even sentences of time, which forced workers onto plantations under wage rates and conditions of employment set by the landlord.[19]

The centerpiece of patronage capitalism was the lien system. Banks and cash were as rare in the South as a pair of matched mules. Therefore, the bureau encouraged the crop lien to answer the need for a system of credit: freedmen might borrow or be advanced seed, fertilizer, tools, shelter, clothing, food, or, more rarely, a little cash by pledging a portion of next year's crop. Labor contracts during Reconstruction revolved around the crop lien.

LABOR CONTRACTS

Labor contracts, signed agreements between landlords and workers whose terms were reviewed by the local field officer of the bureau until it dissolved in 1869, provide the best picture available of capital-labor relations in Louisa during Reconstruction. They reveal the goals of patrons and clients, shed light on landlords' attitudes toward free labor, and document the transition from paternalism to patronage.

On 20 May 1865, eight "former" slaves signed a labor contract with David R. Shelton, their antebellum slavemaster. Shelton agreed to pay Harrison, Fleming, Elihu, Billy, Bob, Lucy, and Judy and her son John for the rest of 1865 "such a part of the crops made on the farm of the said David Shelton the present year (1865) as any I while gentlemen [sic] of the neighborhood shall say is just and right." The workers were to perform whatever tasks Shelton assigned to them "as they formerly did when slaves."[20]

When T. W. Cosby contracted with his former slaves, four men and one woman, he retained the slave custom of "settling up" at Christmas time and other customs too. Servants were to work faithfully until Christmas Day "as in the past," to be fed "in the usual way," and to cultivate and gather the growing crops of all kinds as well as "any other work to be assigned." After deductions for expenses (i.e., food, clothing, and shelter), the servants got one-eighth of the good corn, one-fourth of the Irish and seed potatoes, one-fourth of the cotton and sorghum, but none of the wheat, oats, or hogs.[21]

J. W. Pendleton worked out an arrangement with his nine servants after the war that indicated a more liberal attitude toward his workers than that of Cosby, including an allowance for meat in their payment in kind. For their labor, Pendleton agreed to outfit those who worked outside with clothing at the "end of the year" (December 25), to divide whatever pork remained after providing for feeding of the team, fattening the pigs, and whatever may be eaten. He also agreed to divide all the wheat and oats not used on the farm (except 35 bushels to be set aside for seed and for the purchase of a horse), and all the Irish potatoes and sorghum molasses. His laborers were guaranteed a more varied and nutritious diet as a result of his generosity. A final provision of the contract also revealed a more benign employer; if the servants violated the contract, Pendleton would pay them what any two impartial referees agreed was fair.[22]

Former slaves also signed labor contracts in which making a living was not the only consideration. Such was the case with Martha, who had belonged to Thomas S. Watson before the war. During the war, military action in Louisa County made farming unsafe in certain areas and Watson bought a house and a 2-acre lot for his family in Henry County and rented a plantation. In 1862 he moved his wife, seven children, a niece, a teacher, and slaves to Henry County. By June 1865 this refugee planter wanted to return to his farm in Louisa and Martha also wished to return to familiar territory and reunite with the rest of her family. At Martha's suggestion, Watson agreed to pay her expenses and those of her youngest child in return for her labor as a house servant and maid and the labor of three older children for a period of fifteen days. During this period Martha agreed to search for a home for the three children Watson had temporarily agreed to ration and lodge.[23] Watson also made an arrangement with Eliza Shelton to pay her expenses of moving from Henry County to Louisa in return for her work as nurse and maid "as heretofore she had done" at the rate of $2.50 per month until she worked off the debt of $6.50.[24]

The importance which former slaves attached to the preservation of the family unit is obvious in other contracts and strongly supports recent findings on the strength of the black family under slavery and freedom.[25] In July 1865, Harry Quarles signed a contract with Watson to work under him or an overseer at $7 per month plus rations, minus deductions for time lost due to sickness or for medical bills. Quarles's family was under contract on an adjoining plantation. In order to keep his family intact, Harry Quarles agreed to a contract with Watson which allowed him to break his contract and go with his family if they were forced to leave their farm.[26] Jacob Ragland signed a contract to work for $8 per month which allowed him to keep his mother, rent-free, in one room of his family's cabin and to draw the same ration of 3 pounds of bacon and 1½ pecks of corn meal for her, a ration to which each adult in the household was entitled.[27] Sam Quarles hired his son Albert (ten or twelve years old) and daughter (eight or ten years old) to Watson to feed and clothe "as similar children, hired by others, are fed and clothed in the Green Springs neighborhood." Quarles asked that his children be "brought up in the way they should go," permitting Watson "to inflict moderate and proper chastisement." He further asked that his children be employed "in labor suited to their ages" and treated with kindness.[28]

Planters chose their clients carefully and, like laborers, had definite goals in mind. Thomas S. Watson, for example, rewarded previous loyalty and faithfulness, although grudgingly, in choosing those whose expenses he paid to go back to the Louisa homeplace and be retained as contract laborers. He allowed "Chicken-Yard Lucy" and her son Ben a tenant house on what he called his "Chestnut Forest Place" because she had "nursed his wife" and he had promised to give her a home after slavery. "Now she is claiming that offer and will expect to live here without charges," he lamented. However, Lucy did not want to live in the big house because, according to Watson, "She could not have the same freedom of harboring idle children and grandchildren." He continued, "I would not permit the same vagrancy here they find so delightful there." Reuben, Watson's former carriage driver, was also given a place at "Chestnut Forest," and Watson said he expected "to get something out of him—working my garden, harvesting, etc." Yet he expressed concern that "he will steal and carry off to his family more than the value of his labor." Elizabeth, Watson's wife, complained to her husband about the new cook George Hackett had "highly recommended" but who was no better than those of the past five years.

Freedmen were even forced to make offerings of various kinds as a condition of employment. Eventually, Watson agreed to rent out the land at "Chestnut Forest" only to renters who themselves promised to build their own cabins. Workers who built their houses lived in them rent free, and the cabins remained in Watson's possession even after they had left his farm. Subsequent renters paid rent on these cabins in advance as a condition of long-term employment. The usual rent was $36 per year, with $9 being due when they moved in for the first three months of occupancy.[29] Luther Hughes offered his colt to his landlord, W. J. Winston, and $3 in return for a contract as a farmhand. Winston promised to provide enough oznaburg cloth for a pair of pants and two shirts, serge for a pair of pants and a coat, one pair of brogans, and $3 in wages per month. He would feed and raise the colt and use the animal as long as Hughes worked for him. If the colt shoud die, he agreed to pay Hughes $75, unless

Hughes broke the contract, in which case Winston would assess him $75 in damages.[30]

The kind of contract which Louisa laborers desired most and which planters tried to avert was that which rented a planter's land to a tenant. The field officer for the Freedmen's Bureau in Louisa reported to Washington on conditions in Louisa and described the experience of Louisa's workers. His comments revealed why laborers eagerly sought long-term contracts. Freedmen, he reported, who worked on rented land with necessary means (tools and stock), those who worked for shares, and those who worked by contract did well. However, those without means to work the land, those who worked by the month, and especially those who worked by the day resorted to stealing and "are filling up the jails."[31] The bureau officer in adjoining Culpeper County reported in January 1868 that freedmen preferred the sharecropping contract, which usually gave them one-fourth to one-half of the crops with the farm owner furnishing and feeding the teams. House rent and firewood were often furnished, and provisions were extended for a garden plot and the keeping of pigs and fowls.[32] Tenants also occasionally hired other hands to help them. In nearby Goochland County, the bureau officer noted that laborers on contract, unlike field hands, even managed to save enough to buy a few acres of land.[33]

Planters fretted about renting their land by the year and generally sought to avoid it. Watson's brother-in-law wrote to him in April 1866 complaining that he had been unable to hire hands to work his farm and so he had rented most of it.[34] Watson spoke of "expecting trouble" from "his darkies" before the end of the year (1866) because his renters all wanted to renew their contracts while he hoped that they would "come and go to work—just as they used to do when they belonged to me."[35] Typically, planters offered wage rates of $6–$10 per month, or 25¢ to 35¢ per day.

Thus, Louisa's landlords immediately after the war sought docile and faithful workers for their fields, preferably day hands, at the cheapest wage rates attainable. They provided food, clothing, shelter, land, and sometimes tools, drafted animals, and medical treatment and deducted the costs of these services from the wages allotted to the tenant. Most of the time, no money changed hands until the end of the year and often the tenant had not accumulated wages sufficient to pay advances previously received. In addition to labor, landlords gained capital improvements, such as fences or cabins, at little cost. Finally, their attitude toward free laborers remained possessive; Louisa farmers who had once owned slaves never quite rid themselves of the idea that black labor was theirs.

Tenants sought the reunion of formerly broken families, preservation of the future integrity of the family, chances to work and make a living, economic security in the form of long-term contracts, opportunities for children to learn a trade, the necessities of food, clothing, and shelter, and access to productive factors (land, tools, draft animals, and livestock). Sometimes they secured these ends by expressing individual loyalty or making their own assets available for the landlord's use or agreeing to build their own cabins. Links to the white community had to be made somehow, if black labor was to make a living.

PATRONAGE AFTER 1869

The economic dependence of freedmen upon their landlords, of course, did not end with the folding of the Freedmen's Bureau in 1869. The history of capital-labor relations after Reconstruction is recorded in thousands of transactions in Louisa County deedbooks. Although not as rich and intimate as the bureau records, bonds and deeds of trust document the persistence of the patronage system after Reconstruction.[36]

In 1873 an act of the Virginia General Assembly required agreements for agricultural loans ("advances") to be recorded at county courthouses. The act simply stated that if any person made advances to another person engaged in the cultivation of the soil, the person making the advance was to be entitled to a lien on the crops to the extent of the advances.[37] These laws made it possible for renters to get cash or supplies by borrowing from local lenders. Section 14 stated, "The Lien shall not in any manner affect the rights of landlords to their proper share of rents or right of distress, nor existing liens, nor shall it affect the advancees rights to claim such part of his crops as is now exempt from levy or distress for rent." For example, a renter who had encumbered one-fourth of his crop for rent could not encumber the same one-fourth for any other purpose.

The second part of Section 14 referred to an earlier act of the General Assembly which enabled every householder to set aside up to $2,000 worth of property as exempt from levy or distress from rent, seizure, garnisheeing, or sale under any order or demand for debt. The act was designed to protect debtors from total loss, to prevent them from losing everything they had. This privilege, known as the "Homestead Exemption," had to be claimed, meaning the householder had to go to the courthouse and declare the property he wished to set aside and have it recorded as a deed.[38] This liberal and well-intentioned piece of legislation had little effect in Louisa County. In nearly every deed recording agricultural advances, the debtor waived benefit of the Homestead Exemption. Bedsteads and dressers, hoes and scythes, or livestock were often the only collateral a seeker of credit had. In order to get credit, these items had to be mortgaged too. The deeds which claimed the exemption constituted a small percentage of the total deeds of the county.[39]

On 27 November 1874, Stephen Watson, a black tenant farmer, purchased a yoke of oxen and an ox cart from William Poor, a local landowner-creditor, who had Watson sign a bond for $60, payable in nine months with interest. Jesse Porter, the clerk of court, pledged himself as security for Watson, i.e., acted as "suretor" for the debt, in case he defaulted. Samuel Parsons, another landholder, was appointed "trustee" to sell the oxen and cart if Watson defaulted on his debt.[40]

On 7 January 1873, Stephen Hiter, a black laborer, borrowed $65 from Jacob Gurvits (creditor), a local landowner-attorney, and signed a bond promising repayment. The money was borrowed to purchase a horse. Jesse Porter (suretor) "backed" Hiter for his debt and Samuel Parsons was also appointed trustee to liquidate the collateral pledged by Hiter in case of default: one bay horse, one sorrel horse, one heifer, ten barrels of corn, and his crop of tobacco. Apparently Hiter was a greater risk than Watson.[41]

Garland Butler and T. F. Butler were two white renters of the property of Samuel Parsons, clerk of the circuit court in the 1890s. They were indebted to Parsons for $10.68 for guano, which he had purchased for them for use on his corn and tobacco crop. Parsons agreed to furnish the Butlers seed for the coming year, and, for all these credit extensions, the Butlers conveyed all their claims to the crops they were growing on Samuel's land. The Butlers further contracted to cut, house, and prepare the tobacco crop, to deliver it to the Louisa depot, and to house other crops on the premises until Parsons instructed them to deliver the harvest to his residence.[42]

On 9 March 1903, H. S. Marks, a white laborer, borrowed $85 from John Diggs to be repaid in twelve months with interest. As collateral, Marks lent to Diggs his dark bay mule and one gray horse with the agreement that should Marks default on his debt the animals would belong to Diggs.[43]

In May 1875, Reuben Chiles, a black tenant, signed a note promising to pay George Danne, a local store merchant and landowner, $18.25 plus 6 percent interest. The amount was the cash value of fertilizer advanced to Chiles, who agreed to deliver that part of his tobacco crop sufficient to pay the note. Chiles also agreed to deliver an amount of tobacco sufficient to cover other advances in cash, rations, or purchases at Danne's store.[44]

These deeds exemplify hundreds of similar agreements concluded year after year. A total of 262 such agreements were concluded in 1875 alone, a figure which constituted one-half of all deeds for that year. Formal lien agreements declined to 155 in 1880 and gradually to only 17 in 1900.[45]

These figures, however, cannot be taken as a true measure of the number of encumbering alliances, for several reasons. No thorough record of labor agreements exists after 1869, when the Freedmen's Bureau ceased to operate and oversee labor contracts, although the plantation records of Thomas Watson, state agricultural reports, and the deed themselves indicate a continued hiring of farm laborers. In 1880, for example, Watson wrote to his niece in Alabama and spoke of the family's being in an uproar about Uncle John's deciding to rent his farm out to Negroes. He commented that he felt it was a bad idea.[46] Moreover, arrangements for land access were not always formalized at the courthouse, and perhaps countless other encumbrances were never written down anywhere except in the minds and lives of those involved. Finally, and what is most important: as these sample instruments show, the agreements understated the level of encumbrance because each arrangement often involved, not just two persons, but as many as four in a single transaction.

PATRONAGE AND SOCIAL CONTROL

Three criteria distinguished patron-client coalitions in Louisa labor contracts and deeds of trust between 1865 and 1900: (1) the direction of the coalitions; (2) the complexity of interests; (3) the number of people involved.[47]

Clearly, these were vertical coalitions—cultivators and laborers with economic superiors who controlled the economic resources of the county. Dependent farmers formed vertical coalitions to meet the pressures of unemployment, poverty, and growing families; it was a way to obtain food, clothing, shelter, and work and to gain access to land and credit. Coalitions with fellow clients (horizontal coalitions) offered no incentive when little could be exchanged economically. Unlike peasants of Europe who often owned land and had their own tools and livestock, members of the laboring class of Louisa had little in common beyond misery.

Patron-client coalitions in Louisa were also complex, typically involving multiple interests. Patrons did not seek field hands indiscriminately; they preferred those who were deferential, tractable, and cheap, and who voted right, all in the interest of labor stability, profit, and political hegemony.[48] Clients bargained for work, long-term contracts, credit, surety, factors of production, and food, clothing, and shelter; they were interested in survival, security, and economic advancement.

Of great significance to Louisa's future, however, was the capacity of these liaisons to knit a potentially revolutionary class of landless farmers into the Louisa social fabric, to mediate class conflict. The case of Stephen Hiter above might serve as an example.[49]

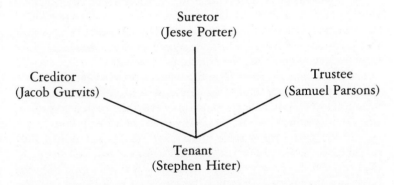

Suretor
(Jesse Porter)

Creditor
(Jacob Gurvits)

Trustee
(Samuel Parsons)

Tenant
(Stephen Hiter)

For the manifestly simple matter of buying a horse, a tenant had to deal with and gain the favor of several different patrons, as Hiter did. Moreover, he also patronized his landlord and local merchants for still other needs, for although the reservoir of wealth was at the top, no single individual could satisfy all the client's needs. Therefore, each client had many encumbering ties with many local patrons, and farmers were locked together in a matrix of creditors, suretors, trustees, and the landlords, with their debtors and renters. For each client, the cost of severing these links was heavy.

For the purpose of analysis, the Louisa social structure might be visualized as a series of lines radiating upward, each representing a link between patron and client. The lines terminate at the top with those who dispense economic favors of all kinds, whether as landlord, merchant, lawyer, or physician. Laborers, tenants, sharecroppers, and small owners cluster at the base. The absence of lines running from side to side indicates the lack of economic exchanges between clients. In Louisa, those at the top dealt individually with the dependent and their families, exchanging economic favors for loyalty and labor and threatening troublemakers with cutoffs of patronage. Unlike debtors, creditors at the top had important horizontal links among themselves as merchants, doctors, lawyers, politicians, and others of the same status level; indeed, creditor and politician or landlord and doctor at times were one and the same person.[50] Together, patrons held a monopoly of all the county's resources, except labor. Moreover, the patronage system met needs of those all up and down the social scale, so there was no sense of urgency to change the system.

More importantly, landlords extracted an unpaid-for surplus in the form of capital improvements, like cabins and fences. One-half to three-fourths of the crops harvested by contractual labor formed another part of the surplus. Livestock were raised from a portion of this surplus and sold in distant markets. Another part of the surplus was invested in bonds and other securities. Such were the ways former slaveowners preserved patrimonial estates.[51]

Only by forging links among themselves could clients have broken the planter monopoly of income-generating factors, and the incentives necessary to such coalitions were undermined by patronage. Louisa farmers had two alternatives: to enter into full participation in the patronage system or to leave the county. When they accepted the terms of patronage, their "choices" had certain consequences. On the positive side, patronage was useful, providing the necessary means of cultivating the land and making a living. Its pernicious effect was to consign the majority to a lifetime of poverty.

III

·

Clients

Clients—who were they, how were they affected by the patronage system, and what were their responses? Clients were farmers of Louisa who depended upon local landlords and merchants for employment, credit, supplies, aid during crises, legal services, and other forms of assistance. Often they needed a "good word," a voucher of support from some benefactor who knew them and would back them in their requests for jobs, loans, land purchases, or help with medical bills or delinquent taxes. Although many Louisans were called "farmers" on the federal population census of 1880, local tax records show many such "farmers" owning little or no property. For example, in 1880 about 80 percent of the "farmer" sample population had less than $100 worth of personal property, and one-half owned no land at all. The federal manuscript census of agriculture for 1880 indicated that some of these "farmers" were tenant farmers. Those "farmers" who could neither be located on local landbooks or the 1880 agricultural census, I have assumed to be agricultural day laborers.[1] I have singled out renters and day laborers in this chapter as primary representatives of Louisa's client class, although small black owners also remained largely dependent upon white landlords, in spite of their success in acquiring land. It is possible to reconstruct the families and household budgets of the client class by combining the agricultural and population censuses, tax records, and local store ledgers. These records also permit an examination of the dynamics of race and class under the patronage system.

Within the client class, racial differences separated the poor from the desperate. Black clients had the least property. While 59 percent of the entire white "farmer" sample owned less than $100 in personal property in 1880, 99 percent of the black sample fell in this category.[2] Racial differences also showed up in the amount of acreage under cultivation, the use of fertilizer and implements, and acreage devoted to food production. White landlords had some control over their allotments to renters and they must have limited them in the case of black labor.

Although it is not entirely clear why blacks' access to productive factors was more restricted, certainly one of the most important reasons was the persistence of racial presuppositions about black labor, many of which had been inherited from slavery, that continued to haunt the black laboring class. Moreover, race and class distinctions, which can be distinguished for the purpose of analysis, were identical in the real world of nineteenth-century Louisa: the black were poor and the poor were black. It seemed a natural correlative that the black were poor *because* they were black. White control over black labor had been justified during the age of slavery in just such racial terms, and patronage, as a surplus-extraction structure, guaranteed the validity of these traditional axioms. Unable to achieve economic independence, freedmen were also unable to shake their identification as servile labor incapable of succeeding without white supervision. Racism in the Emancipation Period was a combination of inherited stereotypes and economic subjugation.

Finally, was economic subordination of the largely black laboring class foolproof? Did black labor resist the patronage system or did their history of accommodation under slavery have a residual effect in the Emancipation Period, as one historian has argued?[3] Were there changes in the power and authority of the patronage system between 1870 and 1900? These, too, are the concerns of this chapter.

DAY LABORERS

Lewis Carter, a thirty-eight-year-old white agricultural laborer, and Deliah, his thirty-year-old wife, were trying to support themselves and two small children in 1870. Their only taxable personal property was a single milch cow, and thus nearly all of their support had to come from Lewis's wages. By 1880, six more children had arrived, and, fortunately, Lewis had managed to buy a horse and several pigs along with some furniture valued under $10. He had also acquired a few hand tools worth almost $10. By 1890, however, the Carter family could no longer be located in the county.

Julius Massey, a thirty-one-year-old black agricultural laborer, and his twenty-seven-year-old wife, Victoria, were struggling to make a living in Louisa in 1870 for themselves and two young children. They owned nothing beyond tables, beds, and chairs, all worth less than $10. By 1880 they had made no gains whatsoever in spite of the need to feed three more children. Unlike Carter, who was fortunate enough to have some livestock, the Masseys were totally dependent upon Julius's wages. Like the Carters, however, by 1890 the Masseys had disappeared from all county records.[4]

Among the client class, day laborers were the most economically insecure, the poorest inhabitants of the county. The sample population turned up 63 black and 47 white laborers, and all but 4 remained in this agricultural status throughout their residence in the county. They stood on the bottom rung of the agricultural ladder. In 1880, nine-tenths ($N = 57$) of the black laborers either held no resources at all or owned property valued at less than $50. Among white laborers, the same was true of nearly two-thirds in the sample.

In 1880, on the average, horses were worth $40, cows $12, and hogs $2 each.[5] The net worth of three-fourths of Louisa's laborers might have been a single horse or less than three cows. It was not horses or cows, however, but furniture—tables, chairs, beds—which was the most common taxable property among laborers. Indeed, among black workers in over one-half of the sample cases ($N = 17$), furniture was the largest component of their property, followed by livestock and draft animals. More white laboring families than blacks held livestock and draft animals, while furniture was the most valuable resource for just over a fourth ($N = 6$) of these families. The poverty of laborers was more difficult to escape because the nature of their holdings made them more dependent upon local patrons and the wages they paid.

Given the wage rates that prevailed in the last third of the nineteenth century, accumulating wealth would have been an extraordinary accomplishment for casual field hands. Wage rates ranged between $5 and $10 per month for black laborers. The 1870 social statistics schedules of the U. S. census reported average wages of farmhands in Louisa of $8 per month if they were hired by the month and boarded. "Boarded" usually meant they took the noon meal on the farm where they worked. The average wages of a day laborer with board was 50¢ per day and 63¢ per day without the noon meal. Female domestic servants in 1870 could expect $2 per week without board.[6] In 1877, wages for farm laborers in Virginia still averaged only $9 per month for men, while women could expect only half as much; both were among the lowest wage rates in the country.[7] In 1874, for example, wage rates for farm laborers elsewhere in the United States averaged $20.00 per month in Maine,

$18.75 in New Hampshire, $17.53 in the western states, and $16.93 in the Middle West.[8] By 1893, wages had changed little, and in Louisa the average wage per month with board was $11, only $3 above the rate in 1870, while the daily rate had climbed only 7¢ in the twenty-three years since 1870, having reached 70¢ per day without board.[9]

A comparison of these wage rates with the cost of living is a difficult but not impossible task. The plain people of Louisa, of course, left no household accounts of their expenses, but shreds of evidence from other sources shed light on their standards of living. W. E. B. DuBois, in a study of the small village of Farmville, Virginia, in 1897, consulted three leading black grocers who maintained accounts for various black families trading at their stores. For a family of five, he calculated the following minimal expenses per week: food, $1.64; fuel, 62¢; clothing, $1.00; rent, 70¢; and miscellaneous, 29¢. Thus an average family of five needed an income of approximately $220 per year to cover basic expenses. Some managed on as little as $175 per year by cultivating gardens and raising a few livestock, and some needed as much as $245 per year.[10]

If one uses DuBois's estimate of $220 and the highest day labor rate of 70¢ per day without board, Louisa's laborers would have had to have worked 314 days a year to support a family of five. Since mean family size over the four decades was 5.5,[11] even this extraordinary effort would have been insufficient. For laborers hired at the highest rate of $11 per month, wages could not have covered minimal expenses for a family of five without additional assistance furnished by the employer, such as food, fuel, rent, or clothing.

Some starved.[12] However, a decline in the costs of food may have averted mass starvation. At Charles Danne's General Store, prices between 1869 and 1900 changed as follows: eggs, 25¢ to 20¢ per dozen; bacon, 25¢ to 10¢ per pound; butter, 25¢ per pound and the same in 1900; flour 6¢ to 3¢ per pound; shoes, $3.00 to $1.40 a pair; and calico, 16¢ to 6¢ a yard. A reduction in the cost of living therefore rescued many family budgets.[13]

Laborers also battled poverty as families. Chapter VI is a full treatment of these efforts. In nearly one-half of black and white unlanded families, wives worked outside the home. Others might have taken in laundry and sewing or performed other tasks for pay, but no record could be found of these activities. Other unrecorded ways of responding to need might have been planting vegetable gardens, hunting and fishing, moonshining,[14] or simply eating less.

RENTERS

Robert Duncan, a forty-seven-year-old white renter, lived with his thirty-five-year-old widowed sister in 1880, along with her seven-year-old daughter and five-year-old son. In 1870, census records showed Robert farming 100 out of the 300 acres he had rented. He owned about $60 worth of machinery and $200 worth of livestock, consisting of one horse and several milch cows and pigs. He was raising corn, wheat, and oats and producing between $200 and $300 worth of farm products in 1870 and was even in the position to hire an outside laborer. By 1880, however, Robert was farming only 70 out of the 300 acres and producing about half of his 1870 output. Instead of a horse, he had gone to oxen, which were cheaper to feed, and he no longer hired an outside laborer. In addition, he had switched to raising Irish potatoes and tobacco and sold most of his machinery. In 1890 Robert had no taxable personal property, after which he disappeared from all records.

Edmund Foy, a fifty-four-year- old black renter, and his sixty-one-year-old wife, Sallie, were farming an indeterminate number of acres in 1870. Some of their children had already left home and they were also caring for several unrelated persons. Unlike Duncan, their white occupational counterpart, the Foys owned nothing beyond a little household furniture. In 1880, Edmund was farming 3 of the 5 acres he had rented. He had 2 acres in sweet potatoes, 2 in wheat, and 1 in tobacco. He owned no draft animals or machinery and had very little help since all of his children were gone by 1880; in addition, the Foys had assumed the additional burden of caring for a nine-year-old granddaughter. By 1890 the family could no longer be located on local records.[15]

The "farmer" sample produced 80 black and 72 white renters or tenants.[16] Renter-clients were clearly in a superior economic position to casual farm laborers. In 1880 about a third of the black ($N = 24$) and white ($N = 25$) renters had no taxable personal property whatsoever, a situation that prevailed among two-thirds to three-fourths of day laborers. Moreover, the renter might draw upon the resources of the employer or use his credit to get necessary

Former Slave Cabins in Louisa County. (Courtesy: Virginia State Library.)

supplies. Most importantly, a tenant had access to land and whatever machinery or draft animals he could coax out of the owner. The relative economic position of renters can be ascertained by looking at their taxable property, observing their records of farm production revealed on the agricultural census schedules, and comparing their progress to that of laborers and owners.

Table 3.1 reveals that white renters were doing quite well in comparison with black renters and in 1880 owned more draft animals and machinery than black farm owners. At least 40 percent of white renters owned machinery and draft animals, compared with 13 percent of black renters. Even more striking, white laborers owned more machinery and work animals than black renters and were, therefore, less enmeshed in the patronage system. Thus, in terms of ownership of productive factors of a long-term income-generating nature, the white renter was comparable to the black landowner and the white laborer was comparable to the black renter.

Table 3.1 Ownership of Productive Factors by Black and White Renters, Laborers, and Farm Owners, Louisa County, 1880

Status(N)	Machinery	Draft Animals
	(percentage)	
Renters		
White (72)	40	44
Black (80)	13	11
Laborers		
White (47)	15	25
Black (63)	6	12
Farmers of 1–100 acres		
White (26)	39	54
Black (28)	29	25
Farmers of 300+ acres (40)	95	92

Source: Personal Property Taxbook, Louisa County, 1880.

Since white renters had greater control over important productive factors of agriculture, it is not altogether surprising to find them cultivating more land than black renters. Forty-three percent of white renters had over 50 acres under cultivation, compared with ony 5 percent of black renters. Census records also revealed that the white renters of the sample applied more fertilizer to their land. In 1880, 43 percent of the white sample ($N = 31$) were applying fertilizer, compared with 17 percent of the black sample ($N = 14$).[17]

Besides growing more crops and using larger amounts of fertilizer, white renters also hired day laborers and, therefore, produced a greater volume of products. Over half of the white sample ($N = 38$) used outside labor, compared with about 10 percent ($N = 9$) of black renters. The value of all products produced, consumed, or sold during 1880 was greater among the white sample, where 56 percent ($N = 40$) produced over $100 worth, compared with 26 percent ($N = 21$) of black renters.[18]

Just as was the case among owners, the principal crops raised by renters were, in order of importance, maize, wheat, and oats, and about 60 percent of both racial groups also grew some tobacco.[19] Since it was solely a cash crop, tobacco formed at least part of the income for renters. Some of the eggs and butter produced on renter farms might also have gone to the owner in the form of rent, though no record of such payments was found.

It is impossible to determine how much freedom the renter actually had in deciding on his crop and livestock mix. It is known that where the two racial groups had complete freedom to decide, such as was the case with family farmers, they raised less tobacco than did the renters. Small farmers could not invest too much in a crop like tobacco, since crop failure might result in a shortage of food and forage. However, since small farmers also raised less corn, wheat, and oats, the decision to grow less tobacco as well may reflect nothing more than the small owner's limited resources.

Swine, chickens, and milch cows were the principal kinds of livestock kept by renters, as was the case among owners. Few raised any sheep, and the milch cow was not widely kept on renter farms, perhaps because of her higher initial cost and the time and expense it would require to grow forage and feed her.[20]

The striking fact is that these initial advantages enjoyed by white renters were not translated into gains of the magnitude experienced by black renters without the advantages. By tracing each renter through the personal property taxbooks for as long as he remained in the county, I could chart the gains or losses each person experienced in the four variables of machinery, livestock, draft animals, or furniture. Among blacks, 59 percent ($N = 39$) of the renters who remained in the county one decade or longer suffered no losses at all in the assessed values of any of these variables. But among whites, only one-third ($N = 18$) preserved or held their own, and 57 percent

($N = 24$) experienced personal property losses during their residence. Thus, in spite of the white renter's larger command of yield-producing factors and in spite of the fact that this made him more productive, he lost lost ground.

Racial differences among renters have several explanations. Census records show that nearly two-thirds of black renter households ($N = 49$) contained members who were employed, compared with less than one-third for white renter families ($N = 22$). The greater utilization of the family as a labor unit among black renters partially accounts for their superior economic advances and their ability to surpass white renters, who initially enjoyed economic superiority. Evidence exists to show that black couples in Louisa waited longer after marriage before having their first child, allowing for a period to get on their economic feet.[21] Other possible explanations may lie in the greater use of credit by the black renter and its potential for making renters more mobile, but this was impossible to determine. Finally, the black renter may simply have been a more efficient farmer for reasons that are unclear.

However, race did determine access to the county's resources. Black renters farmed smaller acreages, raised more tobacco and presumably less food, were limited in their use of fertilizer, and never gained the same control over other productive factors of agriculture as white renters. What explains these racial differences? Employers had control over some of these factors, such as crop-mix, supplies of fertilizer, and acreage allotments. Were black renters more restricted by white landlords than were white renters? If so, why? Was it just another manifestation of the whites' common fear of losing control over their black workforce? The answers to these questions are not entirely clear. Regardless of the explanation for these differences, however, it is important to recognize that class dominance apparently had a racial dimension, even though it may not have been explicit.

RESISTANCE

Clients put their hands to the plow and their feet in the furrow and many neither looked back to see where they had been nor up to see where they were going. The daily grind of marginal farming left little time or energy for serious reflection on the future and how to change it. And why should they ponder these questions? Local leaders were united by their common interests as patrons, and clients, like the muzzled ox who treads out the corn and depends upon his owner to feed him, were muzzled by their poverty. To challenge wage rates, terms of employment, or the quantity and quality of rations and housing would have exposed clients to the risks of never having the muzzle removed. Then, the only alternative would have been migration, uprooting the family and moving into an even more precarious environment. So most endured.

But not all. Patronage was an effective, indeed powerful, form of class domination and labor control, but it was not without weaknesses. The evidence is spotty, but it would be a mistake to ignore challenges to class rule in Louisa. Rather, much can be learned about patronage itself by looking at the evidence of resistance and the forms it took. In spite of their desperation, in spite of their dependency upon landlords, the laboring class found ways immediately after the war to keep patrons honest, to force some measure of equality into the patron-client relationship.

EARLY FORMS OF RESISTANCE

The Freedmen's Bureau officer reported from Louisa in the early months of 1866 that not over one-third of the freedmen had been properly paid for last year's work, and that "the bolder ones" were reacting. Stealing, barn-burning, and mutilating cattle by both freedmen and poor whites were some forms of reaction he mentioned.[22] In the same period the Lynchburg officer noted cases in which freedmen stole from their former masters and also some in the city refused to return to rural areas to work, even in the face of unemployment.[23]

Subtler forms of rebellion also surfaced. As noted above, Thomas Watson talked about "expecting trouble" from "his darkies," about laborers' hesitating to accept his terms of employment and their insisting upon long-term contracts. It is easy to make too much of these sketchy traces of resistance, but, clearly, workers at times made demands of their own and refused to play the role of the happy, obsequious darky.

Migration, or what landlords often referred to as "wandering," was the most obvious expression of resistance.[24] During the Reconstruction period, freedmen denied their labor to local patrons, as streams of former slaves could be seen moving from farms into the nearest city. From Louisa they migrated to the towns and cities of Charlottesville, Richmond, Petersburg, and even distant places like Lynchburg and Roanoke.[25] In places like Lynchburg, Petersburg, Danville, and Richmond they found employment in small tobacco-processing factories. After 1860 village factories declined and the processing of tobacco centered more and more in urban areas. A small tobacco factory at Oaksby, the ancestral home of the Goodwin family, operated during the war. Tobacco was cultivated by slaves, packaged in one-pound bags, and sold as Soldier's Comfort. Charles Goodwin was exempted from the Confederate army because of his large tobacco plantation, and Soldier's Comfort was also furnished to the Confederate army as part of Goodwin's tithes. The Oaksby factory closed in 1864.[26] In 1860 there were 252 small tobacco factories in Virginia located in rural districts; by 1870 only 131 could be found.[27]

In 1866 the Richmond bureau officer estimated that at least 15,000 free blacks had joined the 5,000 who had been slaves in the city before the Civil War. They came without property, without any prior arrangements for employment, and without any support or definite plans, "filling up every cellar and shanty that can afford shelter."[28] They could get higher wages in Richmond, but unemployment was a persistent problem as city tobacco factories usually shut down with the processing of each crop.[29] Yet the movement continued. In 1868 Thomas Watson expressed with irritation his estimate that three-fourths of his servants "had the itch to leave."[30] By the end of Virginia's brief Reconstruction period in 1870, the state as a whole was losing 28 white and 83 black residents per thousand of the population.[31]

Freedmen's open defiance seemed to provoke the same gut-wringing fear as slave rebellion. The Louisa office of the bureau noted in 1867, "Nigger impudency . . . strikes a high-toned terror to the soul."[32] Local patrons responded to these early threats to labor stability—which contractual agreements were supposed to have provided—with their own extraordinary tactics. Louisa's bureau officer reported browbeating, threats to life, and refusals to pay wages. "Whitecapping" was also reported, i.e., driving freedmen from their farms after the harvest season. The threat of whitecapping was also used on workers around election times, to reduce the Republican vote. Local leaders were not above vigilantism. Judge Nelson, a former representative of Louisa County, led a march that drove Thomas Johnson, a black tenant, from the county because he was suspected of burning a local tobacco factory.[33] The Louisa field officer also talked of whites' physically assaulting freedmen when they did not perform work to white satisfaction.[34]

Patrons also took care to prevent black clients from coming together as a group or to limit their activities when they did congregate. Watson's contracts with his Chestnut Forest tenants contained provisions restricting workers from housing any but those whom he approved, and he specifically demanded that tenants keep out all "vagrants."[35] In 1866 a local landowner sold a piece of land near the courthouse upon which stood Ola Methodist Church. The tract and building were to be used for a black congregation of Baptists. Carefully written into the sale agreement were the conditions that the building could be used only for religious purposes and no spirits, wine, beer, or cider could be sold on the premises.[36] In adjoining Madison County, blacks held a parade in which some carried, besides the fife and drum, sabres. When whites became very excited, thinking blacks were organizing a military force, the bureau officer of Madison "instructed" them not to do it again.[37] Any suggestion or organized activity on the part of freedmen raised the same fears which Nat Turner's revolt and John Brown's raid had burned into the minds of Virginians.

At times when class dominance seemed insufficient to control freedmen, threats might take on a racial cast. In Louisa the political ferment of 1867 continued after the election for a short time, as whites were hostile to blacks out of bitterness at the results.[38] Gradually, however, the turmoil subsided, only to resurface in the spring and summer of 1868 as another election drew near. In the first elections after the Civil War, voters in the South faced the most difficult issues in their entire political history, except, perhaps, that of secession. The terms of readmission to the Union, the right of freedmen to vote, and the role of former Confederate officials in postwar politics were some of the more explosive issues. The Madison bureau officer spoke of reports that members of the Conservative party were threatening to drive blacks off their premises if they voted the Republican ticket. The same was true of nearby Culpeper and Goochland counties, and in the latter, Ku Klux Klan placards were posted everywhere in 1868 to frighten and intimidate blacks.[39] In Louisa, Watson reported hearing a lot of talk in 1868 about turning laborers out unless they voted to please employers.[40] He claimed he never engaged in such activity, but his overseer often did "without his authority." In fact, he had told one of the black tenants that if he voted for the constitution (which states had to write to reenter the Union), he felt his rent might go up $10 a month next year. Tenant: "You don't really think so, Mr. Tisdale [white overseer], does you?" Tisdale: "Well, I don't know; but there's a good chance for it." Tenant: "Den sir, I gwine vote like Mass Thomas votes."[41] The Charlottesville bureau officer reported cases of whites' threatening to charge blacks a large fine for taking off to register to vote, and the official informed freedmen that they could only be docked for time lost, scarcely much comfort to hungry freedmen.[42] Thus, when the condition of blacks' economic dependence seemed unable to assure a continuation of white economic and political domination, the white elite were not above marshalling the balder forces of race.

RESISTANCE—1869–1900

Resistance after 1869 continued, and, like that during Reconstruction, was sporadic, infrequent, and noncollective. According to courthouse records which may not be the complete record of violent resistance, between 1870 and 1900 the incidence of felonious crime averaged just over two felonies per year, or a total of 69 serious crimes over three decades.[43] Over two-thirds of these crimes came under the categories of housebreaking, larceny, tobacco-house burning, and assault.

State and nationwide movements of farm protest offered poor farmers in Louisa County opportunities for protest, but there is no evidence that they were effective in rallying the poor. Instead, for reasons that are unclear, the movements were led by those mostly "among the Virginia aristocracy," severely limiting their radicalism. The Farmers' Assembly was organized in 1885 in Richmond and elected as its first president Robert Beverley, a large landowner "of ancient lineage,"[44] The Southern Farmers' Alliance organized in Texas in the 1870s but got a late start in Virginia. It held its first meeting in Luray in 1888 and at its peak had 113 suballiances and 30,000 members. In Virginia, the president was Major Mann Page and, according to one account, there was "a no more aristocratic Virginian." The "equally Patrician Colonel Randolph Harrison" edited the state Alliance's official paper.[45] Alliance leaders varied from state to state, but the leaders of Virginia "bore the names Page, Beverley, Cocke, Ruffin, Harrison—than which there were none more honored."[46] Not surprisingly, the Alliance in Virginia appealed mostly to farm operators, not laborers.[47] The Farmers' Assembly expired shortly after 1890, but the Alliances, North and South, merged in 1892 into the People's party, commonly called Populists. General James G. Field, a former Confederate commander, became the vice presidential candidate. After defeat at the national level, Virginia Populists ran a candidate for governor in 1893 who lost largely as a result of the success of the Democrats in portraying the candidate as soft on race.[48]

Participation in collective movements of this nature offered little hope to the laboring class, and migration continued to be the most visible form of resistance and between 1880 and 1900 it increased. In Virginia, white out-migration inched up slightly to 32 per thousand in 1890, but the black rate rose from 83 to 115 per thousand between 1870 and 1890.[49] In the 1880s the black population of Louisa declined by one-fifth and, between 1880 and 1900, 2,910 blacks left the county. In 1860 Louisa's blacks made up 62 percent of the population, but by 1900 they were 52 percent of the total. The greatest population decline came in the 1880s, when the black population dropped by 18 percent and the white by 3 percent.[50]

Laborers and renters were the most likely to leave the county, and the most stable group were freedmen who acquired land. Using the Louisa personal property taxbooks to obtain a sampling at decade intervals for measuring persistence, I was able to determine that 60 percent of the day laborers from the sample population remained in the county less than a decade; the same was true of about 21 percent of renters. Among blacks who became landowners, 71 percent stayed in the county over a decade, a rate even greater than the 60 percent rate for white owners. Also, the black tenant persisted longer than the white tenant in the sample population. In sum, migrants were most likely to be those without property.

EROSION OF PATRONAGE

Other forces combined with resistance to loosen the grip of patrons over clients and erode the patronage system. The most dramatic development was the success among freedmen in the county in acquiring land. In 1870 black owners constituted only 2 percent of all landowners, but by 1900 they made up 39 percent of the total. A 10 percent random sample of the entire Louisa population taken from the 1900 manuscript census of population produced

150 black heads of household.[51] Since the Louisa landbook in 1900 indicated 1,314 black landowners, about 88 percent of all black heads of household in 1900 owned land![52]

Former slaves became landowners in a variety of ways, but not without the help of local patrons. In 1884 Thomas Watson sent his son to Chestnut Forest place looking for a black hand said to be "trying to steal some of our land up there."[53] The report of his findings, however, was not recorded, and no further references to land stealing were made. Most of the land appears to have been purchased through various loan arrangements. Lewis Ragland, Watson's former slave, sold a piece of land he owned to Billy Mitchell, also a former slave. In 1884, Ragland wrote to Watson from Arkansas, where he had gone to find work, and asked Watson, whom he addressed as "Master Thomas," to "get my money—I need it—then you can take your money and send me the rest." In a subsequent letter, Ragland stated he had received Watson's reply and that he knew it would cost him to get his money, but he needed it to buy another place. He was willing to pay Watson for getting it. In 1892 Ragland asked again about the money "coming to me" from the house and lot he had sold to Mitchell.[54] In another case, Shadrack Johnson bought land with Watson acting as trustee, whereby Watson collected the money from Johnson, paid the person to whom Johnson was indebted, and collected a fee for his service.[55] Nat Ragland also had an account set up through Watson in 1893 for land he sold to Peter Homes (sometimes Holmes), also Watson's former slave. It was a 19-acre plot that Ragland had previously purchased from William Bruce. Homes paid $6 an acre on a three-year note, plus 6 percent interest. Watson kept an account of the sporadic payments, sometimes in cash, sometimes in the form of livestock, until the loan was paid. In this case, Watson apparently acted as the lender and accountant and received the 6 percent interest for his services.[56]

However, too much should not be made of land as a measure of black independence. According to the sample population, these were not great estates, but petty holdings which averaged 24 acres. Moreover, as Chapter I noted and as examples there show, land ownership did not guarantee independence of local patrons. Small owners in Louisa continued to rent or work out as day laborers. Moreover, for blacks, ownership came at great family sacrifice and land acquisition was not accompanied by similar gains in other yield-producing factors. Indeed, a cow or ox at times had to be forfeited for payment, as was the case with Peter Homes above. Black owners still were dependent upon patrons and most remained mired in poverty. Finally, the land they did manage to acquire was not the best in the county, and Louisa land overall was of poor quality. In 1899 the state auditor found land owned by blacks in Louisa worth $2.86 per acre and that of whites to be worth $3.49 per acre. A federal soil survey of 1905 found Louisa's soil to rank at the bottom of Virginia Piedmont soils in humus content.[57] Nevertheless, freedmen had gained a toehold in the county and acheived some independence from local landlords.

When class rule seemed to be weakening, racism reared its ugly head, just as it had earlier during the Reconstructuion period. The same deterioration in race relations accompanied the economic progress of freedmen after Reconstruction. The South in general capitulated to racism in the 1890s in the form of Jim Crow laws. Beginning with Mississippi in 1890, state after state called constitutional conventions ostensibly for the purpose of improving their Reconstruction constitutions. In each case, provisions were taken to disfranchise blacks and carve loopholes into the disfranchising provisions through which poor whites could slip.[58] Virginia was no different in this regard; its convention lasted from 1901 to 1902.[59] Without county newspapers, Louisa left no traceable record of Jim Crowism, but it would be extraordinary if the county had bucked the state and regional trend. The economic progress of blacks in the county, their growing independence, and their out-migration were certainly causes for alarm. The papers of Thomas Watson show that he expressed his concern, as he made a shift to dairy farming, which, as the following chapter will show, was a reaction by many patrons to labor problems.

POVERTY AND RACISM

One of the costs of the patronage system was poverty, and Louisa's clients paid most of the bill. Growing families and low wages limited their capacity to escape its consequences through hard work, thrift, and savings. The patronage system provided their only access to land, tools, credit, and work, and its cost was encumbering debt and the mortgaging of their futures to patrons. Most were unwilling to raise these costs by openly challenging the system. In addition, the majority refused to uproot their families for the slums of cities like Richmond. They therefore tried to mitigate its effects; women and children worked, budgets were carefully watched, gardens cultivated, and diets no doubt supplemented by hunting and fishing. A remarkable number of freedmen managed to acquire property. A significant minority was willing to challenge class rule, make demands upon planters, and even resist through arson, thievery, or violence. However, most resistance took the form of migration. This movement began after the Civil War, grew gradually until about 1880, and approached 20 percent of the population between 1880 and 1900.

The reaction of patrons to these developments will be covered more completely in the following chapter, but, as noted above, threats to class rule periodically brought outbursts of racism. Racism was always latent in Louisa and its ebb and flow after the Civil War related to the social structure and its changes, not to intellectual ferment in the county.

During slavery, planters had understood slowdowns, loafing on the job, or feigned illness in racial terms, as signs of laziness or the everlasting need of black labor for white supervision, not as expressions of resistance to class rule. Slaves, of course, could not effectively challenge these stereotypes by individual economic achievement so long as they were confined to work under white control. Therefore, the stereotypes persisted and evolved into an ideology.[60]

Racial stereotypes inherited from slavery continued to be applied to freedmen. Moreover, arguments were borrowed from the stereotypes of the past to specify a natural position for former slaves as sweated labor in the fields of white farmers. The first report of the Virginia commissioner of agriculture made the following observations on capital-labor relations in 1877:

> It has become the custom to see the negro as shiftless and lazy. But if he is promptly and fairly paid, enough good ones can be obtained to till our farms. We must not abuse him but elevate and encourage him. We have to use the negro at present and have no choice. Suppose it were practicable to employ white laborers—that we had money enough to pay them double what we have to pay the negro—to afford them lodgings doubly as expensive as what the negro is content with—to give them flour in place of corn bread, and that we could get from them double the labor we can get from the negro (which is a mere hypothesis) then what will become of the negro? They have to be supported some way and southern farmers need laborers they can superintend, watch and direct. It is a disadvantage for a farmer to have a laborer who thinks he knows more than his employer. The farmer must be able to direct the movements of the laborer. The negro has been raised to obey. Not so with the white man.[61]

Two years later and a decade and a half after slavery, the commissioner emphasized again his view of the proper order of things when he pointed out that white laborers were not satisfactory field hands because they were "not in the habit of working in fields all day"; they were also harder to please, wanted more, and "think they know more." He claimed that the present generation of colored laborers were harder to control, but they could be trained.[62]

Thomas Watson's daughter revealed her contempt for black labor in different but unmistakable terms. Writing to her mother in 1884, she complained that she had changed her cook and nurse every month for the past six months. "I am actually disgusted with house-keeping and the colored race! Father's pets! My cook now is a stupid *animal* and I have her girl, 12 years old, for nurse and house maid . . . both have the coarsest African cast of features and manners. The real *savage* comes out all the time. Finally, she expressed her disgust over her nurse's bad work habits, that she just "took off" all the time, most recently for a "baptizing."[63]

Since most Louisa freedmen remained poor, unable to advance toward a class of prosperous, self-sufficient farmers, their poverty continued to be the wellspring of racism. It was not simply the ideology inherited from slavery which cursed Louisa and its black population, but the persistent poverty of freedmen combined with this intellectual legacy. Unable to achieve economic independence and freedom from white domination, the black poor had little chance to convince patrons that the "itch to leave" was not a sign of laziness and indolence or that their poverty was not a racial charac-teristic but a form of racism. To employers of black labor, black poverty and white economic hegemony were elements in the natural order of things.

A most explicit statement of Virginia's belief in caste and class distinctions as the mooring posts of social order appeared in a Richmond newspaper in 1882. "The true teaching is that both 'caste' and 'class' must exist in all organized society, and their abolition, admitting such a thing possible, could result in nothing else but a return to primitive barbarism." The editor went on to acknowledge that Thomas Jefferson had established "equality by birth" in the Declaration of Independence, but caste and class distinctions had grown. And the "best government in the world was the rule of the best people." The highest aspirations for the rest must be within their own caste and class.[64]

IV

·

Patrons

Labor difficulties, growing numbers of black landowners, and migration combined with the problems of soil depletion, low yields, and agricultural depression to challenge the economic security and hegemony of Louisa patrons. Instead of promoting labor stability and prosperity, the patronage system had provoked class conflict and poverty, and these had become new forces for change. Poverty and class cleavage not only threatened class rule but the continued profitability of plantation-style agriculture. How patrons adjusted to threats to their status is the subject of this and the following chapters. Were Louisa's former slaveowners wedded to a past of labor-intensive agriculture or did they respond to profit incentives and alter their agricultural practices?

In 1880 Louisa County had 1,895 freeholders. The "farmer" sample of 1880 produced 113 white and 28 black owners, and they have been traced through federal and local records at decade intervals between 1870 and 1900. The federal agricultural schedules of the manuscript census in 1870 and 1880 provided much detail on the individual farmer's allocations of acreage to specific crops and production figures, and local land and personal property tax records supplied the monetary value of machinery, draft animals, livestock, and furniture. Tax records revealed the distribution of factors of production in 1870, 1880, 1890, and 1900 and provided snapshots of each farmer's gains and losses at these intervals. These records made it possible to examine agricultural practices of freeholders of various farm sizes.

For the purpose of analysis, sample freeholders have been divided into three categories: those holding 1–100, 101–300, and 301 or more acres. Farmers of 100 acres or less represent the small farm, and the level of technology during the late nineteenth century made farming possible on this scale with family labor alone.[1] The 101–300 acre farm represents the middling farmer who produced a surplus above household needs; those holding over 300 acres represent the wealthiest farmers, who produced the greatest surpluses of farm products. The sample population of 1880 included 54 small, 47 middling, and 40 large farmers.[2]

SHIFT TO GRASS FARMING

A shift to dairying, livestock, and grass farming characterized Louisa landowners who owned more than 100 acres. The change was gradual and is difficult to date but it began soon after the Reconstruction era, grew steadily in the 1870s, and accelerated in the 1880s. It was triggered by labor difficulties, farm price trends, soil depletion, and urban demands for food. In 1869, Thomas Watson, who owned 945 acres of farm land at "Brackets," wrote to a friend, "I am trying to raise corn, wheat, and tobacco, but have failed so that I am considering turning my Green Springs land into a grazing farm. I bought $150 of grass seed the other day." By 1876 he had a large dairy producing "lots of butter and milk."[3] He was also selling lambs and mutton in Richmond, and the main crop was now grass.[4]

In 1880, Watson decided to try a silo and had one built to see how it would work. After the first year he was ecstatic, writing to a friend, "Tell the major that as sure as corn will grow in Alabama, an unlimited amount of winter provender may be saved—at a cost so trifling that it seems incredible." He decided to quadruple the silos the following year.[5] In the same year he sent his son to New York to buy "the very best implements and then we will show the Green Springs how to do high farming."[6] In 1881 he ordered two new harrows and made plans for more.[7]

Watson continued to expand his grass-farming practices. In the winter of 1884 he opened another underground silo to feed thirteen beeves, in addition to his milch cows. Soon Watson began to be consulted as an expert on his progressive farming practices. H. M. Magruder wrote to him from Charlottesville inviting him to a club meeting to talk about his underground silo and how to keep ensilage from spoiling. James Holladay, another Louisa farmer-friend, wrote and asked Watson's advice on how to increase supplies of forage for stock feeding and manure, noting that Watson had outdone others in making ensilage work. Holladay also noted that he grew his first corn for ensilage purposes in 1880. Watson had interest in other stock

"Bracketts"—Home Estate of the Watson Family.   (Courtesy: Virginia State Library).

than cattle; sheep sheared at Bracketts in 1896 produced 502 pounds of wool; eggs were also shipped from his farm for sale.[8]

The number of milch and beef cattle, sheep, and swine grew rapidly in Louisa County in the 1870s. Milch cows increased by 1,000 from about 2,300 to 3,300, beef cattle from 1,600 to 3,300, and sheep and swine nearly doubled. The production of eggs and butter showed a marked rise. After 1870 and for the rest of the century, the shift to grass farming continued. By 1895 Louisa had slightly more land in pasture than the state average, and dairying in the county was still on the increase; acreage devoted to hay and maize rose while wheat and oats declined.[9] In 1870 Louisa had 886 acres in hay and 7,600 in corn; in 1900 the county had 5,000 acres in hay and about 24,000 acres in corn.[10]

Tobacco growing also rose after the war but the increase did not signal an increasing dependence upon this staple. Acreage in tobacco increased from 1,162 acres in 1870 to 2,647 in 1900. Much of this rise resulted from the entry of numerous small farmers into the market. Large owners, of course, continued to grow tobacco, but few increased the acreage in this troublesome, labor-intensive staple. In 1880, for example, Watson raised no tobacco whatsoever.[11]

Actually, the decline in the quality of Louisa's tobacco and the importance of this staple in the local economy was part of a broader trend affecting tobacco throughout the state. In 1880 the overproduction of poor tobacco in Virginia was a "serious problem." The commissioner of agriculture called upon Virginia farmers to give up tobacco-farming and replace it with stock raising.[12]. Many farmers followed his advice. By 1887 the area planted in tobacco in Virginia, Tennessee, and Kentucky was "greatly reduced" because of the effects of low prices and contamination from poor handling and processing by small growers.[13] In 1894 Virginia's tobacco crop was valued at less than half the value of any crop since 1880, except 1888.

Moreover, technological change combined with a shift of consumer taste to cigarettes and the success of tobacco entrepreneurs in the Carolinas to move the center of the tobacco culture southward. In spite of the invention in 1880 of a cigarette machine by James A. Bonsack, a Virginia teenager, the state lost out to the marketing talents of enterprising tobacconists in North Carolina.[14]

The shift to grass farming diminished the need for hired labor, especially among large farmers. Farmers of over 300 acres were always the greatest employers of labor, and they were in the best financial position to make the shift to grass farming. Among the 40 sample farmers with over 300 acres in 1880, about three-fourths had used hired labor during the previous year; two-thirds of those with 101–300 acres had used hired labor.[15] Timolean G. Trice, for example, spent between $100 and $200 for labor in 1870 on his farm of 439 acres. However, in 1880 he spent between $26 and $50 on 413 acres. During this period he reduced the amount of acreage in tobacco, increased his acreage in hay and pasture, and bought more sheep.[16] In 1895 the labor market in Virginia agriculture was described as "steady" for skilled laborers "like dairymen, poultry-men, stockhandlers and men experienced in the use of improved implements and machinery," but declining for unskilled hands.[17] The move to grass farming away from wheat, oats, and tobacco among patron-farmers meant that fewer tenants and field hands had to be hired.

Thomas S. Watson employed a milcher and washer for his dairy in 1884 and a hand to tend the chickens, all relatives of Harry Quarles, a former slave of his. The milcher and washer was the daughter of Harry Quarles, "who used to belong to me." He already had Judy and Mildred Quarles, sisters of his new dairy helper, in his employ as cooks. He also hired Lam Quarles, a first cousin to Judy and Mildred, to feed his chickens; Watson felt Lam was too big for the job but was "cheap." Harry wanted Lam to work for Watson because he felt he would be "cared for, treated, and looked after when sick." Harry Quarles was present at the hiring of Lam and Watson related a humorous incident: "I looked all over Harry, and his waistcoat being open, I saw my own name on the waistband of the white shirt which he wore! Harry owes me for the land on which he lives—a negro who can read, a neighbor of Harry's stood near, I called his attention to my brand on Harry's shirt . . .! He guffawed and said, 'Mas Thomas if he don't pay you, sell him—sir—sell him—no matter what the Yankees say,—he wearing your clothes and living on your land yet!' This was quite a treat to me!"

AGRARIAN CAPITALISM

Grass farming helped solve the problem of labor uncertainty, but the shift to dairying and poultry raising was motivated by the drive for profit too.[19] The demand for dairy and poultry products rose as the urban populations of Washington, D. C., Baltimore, Philadelphia, New York, and Richmond expanded.[20] By 1889 Orange and

Spotsylvania, two counties which adjoined Louisa, had built local creameries to capitalize on the growing urban demand for dairy products.[21] Dairying "accelerated" in 1889, especially in Virginia counties close to these urban centers, and was described as "greatly increased" in 1891 and "still increasing" in 1899.[22] In 1893, 1,800 pounds of dressed turkeys were shipped from Trevillian's railroad depot in Louisa County, and the return was "better than anything else on the farm."[23] In 1895 poultry and poultry products constituted "one of the largest industries in Virginia."[24]

Most of the surplus generated by the surplus-extraction structure of patronage was exported from Virginia, and some of it was marketed outside the United States. In 1880 Thomas Watson debated about shipping his muttons to Baltimore or Richmond. He decided on Baltimore because "Richmond is a onehorseplace with 80,000 inhabitants, half of which are Negroes that eat saltfish, rusty bacon, etc., no high priced fresh meats." He noted that it was a common practice to ship to Europe, bragging to a friend that Mr. Beverley of Fauquier County "had sent to England 400 beeves, 800 muttons the other day." Watson's son, Thomas S. Watson, Jr., and Robert Beverley, son of the Fauquier farmer, were classmates at Virginia Military Institute in Lexington, Virginia. In May 1880, Robert wrote to Thomas S. Watson, Jr., that "after leaving Lexington I was connected as you are with my father in farming for three years, principally raising cattle. All my father's cattle 500–600 were marketed chiefly in Baltimore." He continued that his father also shipped 150 head to Liverpool, England, "last fall," and since then "many others to Europe." He concluded that he was now living in Rappahannock County on an estate of 3,000 acres that his father owned and was "dedicated to farming."[25] Other correspondence revealed Watson selling stock to cattle dealers in New York.[26] In 1899 the Virginia commissioner of agriculture reported the state's failure to supply even half the "home demand" for butter and cheese; much of it being exported outside the state, where it commanded higher prices.[27] Even after paying freight charges, farmers like Watson and Beverley apparently could more profitably market their produce outside the state.

The drive for profit in the form of exporting the agricultural surplus was intensified by the agricultural depression. Prices for wheat, corn, and tobacco, which had been the principal crops of Virginia since colonial times, plunged between 1866 and 1896. Wheat, selling for $2.31 per bushel in 1866, was bringing 68¢ per bushel in 1896; corn went from 89¢ per bushel to 34¢; bright tobacco that was selling for $13.32 per pound in 1875 would bring only $6.46 in 1896.[28] Other farm products, including dairy and poultry products, followed the same trend, although the drop was not quite as severe for these staples: bacon dropped from 17¢ per pound in 1866 to 10¢ in 1896; butter declined from 25¢ per pound in 1870 to 14¢ in 1896; eggs dropped from 21¢ per dozen in 1866 to 14¢ in 1896. No relief came until 1896 when farm prices began to rise, a trend that continued until the end of World War I.

Like the South as a whole, Louisa's large farmers also attempted to boost crop yields by using more fertilizer.[29] Among the sample population, 38 and 63 percent of the middling and large farmers, respectively, used fertilizer in 1880, compared with 7 and 31 percent of black and white small farmers, respectively.

Besides altering their agricultural practices and attempting to get more out of the same piece of land, patron farmers strove to improve their financial position by shifting their investments, selling small parcels of their land, and even migrating from the county. Thomas Watson had $10,870 invested in bonds in 1870 on which he paid a personal property tax of $5.73. Money, stocks, and bonds were taxed at very low rates, and one way of avoiding taxes was to use these shelters. Robert Kent, the county's largest landholder, had $25,000 invested in securities in 1899. The use of tax shelters like these was notorious in the state. In 1883 the commissioner of agriculture noted their widespread use and complained that "this causes the class upon whom the burden chiefly falls to likewise dodge the assessor."[30] Farmers shifted their investments in still other ways. One of Watson's planter friends invested $580 in a threshing machine, which he rented out with "some profit."[31] In some cases, investment income covered all farm costs. In 1881 Watson debated about building silos because of the expense of construction. In his ruminations he fretted, "The farm nets nothing and I live off the interest. Recently, I have had to dip into the principal."[32]

Selling small parcels of large estates might also provide cash for other uses. Charles Danne, a slaveholder, owned about 570 acres of land before the Civil War. In 1880 he rented out his land. He had also established a general store and was one of Louisa's local merchants. Between 1880 and 1899 he sold 114 acres and continued to rent the remainder. Between 1870 and 1900, 60 percent of the farmers who owned between 101 and 300 acres in 1870 sold small parcels of their land, and 53 percent of those with over 300 acres showed decreases.[33] Livestock could also be sold for small amounts of cash, but it proved impossible to discern whether reductions resulted from sale, slaughter for personal use, or death of the animals.

For some, the restless search for profit ended in leaving the county for unknown destinations. Thomas Watson, Jr., writing to his cousin in Alabama, remarked that neighbors Reuben and Walker Mackie, their children, and their children's children had all said they were all going to sell out and move to Texas, where they had relatives.[34] About one-third of the sample landowners of the middling and one-third of the large farms disappeared from the personal property taxbooks between 1870 and 1900.

PATRONAGE CAPITALISM

The claim that the South did not take the capitalist path "to modern society" during the last third of the nineteenth century, that the planter class refused to move away from labor-intensive farming, introduce stock raising, or substitute machinery for tenant labor has no basis in fact in Louisa County.[35] Indeed, the opposite was the case. Louisa's planter class responded to the growing urban and even foreign demand for meat and for dairy and poultry products, shifting to poultry and livestock raising and grass farming. The shift was gradual but nevertheless dramatic, beginning after Reconstruction and continuing to the end of the century. Louisa's agricultural transformation was not unique. Other Virginia counties had begun the shift before the Civil War, and the trend continued after the war.[36] Thus, the vigor of agrarian capitalism in Louisa represented a broader pattern across the state; Virginia planters were attuned to the profit incentive.

The alternative suggestion has been made that the New South might best be seen as an "evolving bourgeois society" in which a capitalist social structure was rising on the ruins of a premodern slave society.[37] Although this description is closer to what was happening in Louisa, it is somewhat misleading. Misleading, because it implies a discontinuity between the two Souths when the most essential feature of both slave Louisa and Emancipation Louisa was class rule. Louisa's slaveowners built great estates, invested in bonds and other securities, and altered their farming practices to meet market pressures. Slavery made the accumulation of wealth possible. After the war, the same planters prospered, shifted assets, and farmed for profit; heavily encumbered freedmen and poor whites made these things possible. In both cases, the social structure remained essentially unchanged, and capitalism had not evolved but merely changed forms. Only the labor system had changed, and the patronage system guaranteed that legally free labor would not destroy the economic basis of class rule.

Patronage capitalism rescued the planter class. Grass farming solved in one stroke the problems of soil depletion, labor uncertainty, and low profit. Hay, clover, and other leguminous crops began to restore the humus content of the soil; reduction of crop farming reduced the need for labor. Large planters like Thomas Watson used the interest of investments to cushion the loss of slave property and buy time for readjustment; he suffered little in the agricultural transformation. The shift to grass farming boosted his profits and allowed him to increase his capital assets.

Watson's economic success permitted him to own a retreat house in Richmond, and he was able to loan his son $8,931 in 1890 to buy 856 acres in the fertile Green Springs district. He was even a lender to another patron in 1884. Henry J. Wale got a short-term loan of $100 from Watson to feed and employ his hands. In 1896, Watson passed about $7,300 in stock and bonds along to his daughter as her share of his father's estate.[38] His portion was not noted. As the following chapter will show, his taxable wealth in the county remained substantial.

The planter class after the war remained a self-conscious elite. This is evident, of course, in the consideration and attention Watson gave to financial dealings of all kinds. However, it was also apparent in other ways. In 1887, for example, Thomas Watson's papers show an intense, year-long concern over tracing the family genealogy. After writing scores of letters to relatives, he finally attempted to write a history of the Watson family, tracing its ancestry to Scotland. Family members who had achieved distinction got elaborate attention, finally, in an incomplete and poorly written history. The self-consciousness of the planter class was also apparent when Watson's son wrote his cousin, living in Alabama, in 1884 and told her about recent weddings in the county. He related that Frank Saunders, son of Bolling, married a girl who was "considered something of an heiress." She was the granddaughter of Charles Danne, the local merchant. Young Watson continued, "I had my eye on her but too much of a laggard. I fear I will never get an heiress."[39]

Louisa's patrons felt the effects of economic depression, of course, but unlike clients, who made sacrifices, planters made adjustments.

The adjustments of patron farmers consisted of liquidating some of their assets like land, buying more fertilizer, or moving to greener pastures. In 1869, Watson talked in still other terms of the changes which the new order required of those like himself. He complained that hard times were forcing him to send his son to Virginia Military Institute instead of Switzerland for an education.[40]

Finally, the marketing of the surplus of farm produce outside of Louisa County while workers who produced the surplus struggled to feed themselves is convincing proof that the surplus-extraction structure profited the patron at the expense of the client class. The state commissioner of agriculture noted in 1889, "The old idea of the colored laborer is giving way to a concern on the part of the planter for the money value of all that comes from his land."[41] His comments suggest that labor was treated more harshly as the economic depression deepened, which would not be unexpected. Under patronage capitalism, labor constituted a commodity cost of production. As costs in general rose and cut into planter profits, the interests of capital and labor became even more antithetical. To lower costs, planters moved away from long-term labor contracts, which provided for food, clothing, shelter, and medical expenses, and toward the use of casual day labor hired on an ad hoc basis and guaranteed nothing beyond a day's pay.

V
.

Patronage Politics

In a recent essay, Harold D. Woodman challenged economic historians to view the market as a total political, economic, and social system. Class relations, violence, and intimidation cannot be ignored, he argued, simply because they defy measurement. In this broader perspective, the market is potentially a "vehicle" for exploitation and control.[1] I have already analyzed Louisa's economic and social system as a set of exploitative class and caste relationships. The political system also became a vehicle of exploitation. Indeed, the political system was nothing more than an extension of the economic system that sustained it. The landed elite dominated life at the courthouse. They occupied all the appointive offices and, through various manipulations such as gerrymandering and favoritism, won election to the few elective positions. Once in office, these holders of power used the treasury as a wellspring of patronage politics, extracting funds in the form of taxes from the poor and dispensing them in the form of fee payments to the wealthy for services which they were appointed to perform.

Political patronage was comparable to economic patronage. Since it squeezed a surplus from the client poor, in this case in the form of taxes, and channeled it into the hands of the patron rich, it was the extension of class rule into the courthouse. Since all of the officeholders and administrative staff were white, most of whom were former slaveholders harboring prewar prejudices about the black population, it was also an extension of race or caste rule into the courthouse. Unlike economic patronage, however, political patronage brought few benefits to the client class beyond meager payments of welfare to avert starvation or coffins the county furnished to bury the indigent dead. During the political turmoil surrounding Reconstruction Louisa's politicians realized the increased importance of local politics. It was also during this period that poverty emerged as a formidable problem and a serious threat to social order.

67

In 1868 during the midst of the controversy over Reconstruction in Virginia, Thomas S. Watson stated categorically, "As I fought the Radicalism of N. England to preserve the Slave power (which I esteemed of inestimable value), I am convinced that the loss of that issue by battle makes it impossible . . . to raise any other issue that could eventuate in good to us." For Watson it was rather pointless to "thwart the plans of the North"; after all, he lamented, Reconstruction did not pertain "to the *South that I loved.*"[2] Watson's expression about the irrelevance of national politics was a common attitude among southern planters after the Civil War. Economic survival had become their "first priority."[3]

The "disengagement of planters from national politics," however, was only a sensible withdrawal from the politics they had little chance of affecting. Planters did not intend "to forfeit meekly their power," which would have jeopardized their dominance of the economic and social structure. According to a recent study of the planter class during this period, "Because politics and plantations were still linked, . . . the battle to preserve plantation agriculture and planter power became a political as well as an economic affair."[4] It was to the local level that planters shifted their attention and it was here that they waged their campaign to retain control over political and economic affairs. Here they could make a difference. Here they could practice the politics of patronage.

The courthouse was the center of public life in nineteenth-century Louisa.[5] Physically, it was a smaller building than the imposing structure of today, which was enlarged in the early twentieth century, enclosed by a fence, and accentuated by a monument to the Confederate dead, with a soldier, rifle in hand, facing toward Washington, D. C.[6] Notices on the older building's doors proclaimed what was about to be decided inside or what had already been decided. Unless a marriage, birth, or death was to be recorded, a will or deed made out, or a homestead exemption claimed, ordinary folk had no reason to enter. Of course, common folk could be rather harshly introduced to its inner workings if they violated the law, but for the most part they learned of the great decisions affecting their lives by reading the door. Delinquent tax lists, trial dates, and announcements of public auction of the property of those who had not paid their taxes were posted here, as were reports, for example, of the decision of the Board of Supervisors to raise taxes or require residents to fence in their livestock.[7] Thus, the courthouse held the purse strings of the county, and whoever controlled the courthouse ruled Louisa.

Louisa County Courthouse—Old and New. (Courtesy: Virginia State Library.)

The most immediate and pressing problem for Louisa's postwar leadership was the destination of thousands of former slaves. Poverty in the county put great strains on Louisa's budget, now more limited as the result of the loss of slave revenues. More important for the planter class, indigence posed some serious risks. Unless relief to the poor was extended, the planter class faced spreading discontent and potential challenges to their authority. On the other hand, relief expenses had to be contained if there was to be anything left for election expenses, salaries, and the general administrative costs of county government. Since planters hoped to control local government, tax money was necessary for these expenses too, else their political power could be jeopardized. The question of responsibility for the poor, church or state, was an historical issue. In resolving it, earlier generations discarded a benevolent, nonpartisan, and intimate solution for a harsh, political, and bureaucratic welfare system.

BACKDROP

Poverty first became a problem for Virginians late in the colonial period. In 1755 the General Assembly of Virginia was forced to deal with an expanding number of colonists incapable of supporting themselves. An act of that assembly began with the acknowledgment, "whereas, the number of poor people hath of late years much increased throughout this colony . . ." and concluded by directing parishes to establish workhouses. In the workhouse, Virginians invested great hope, not only for alleviating poverty by employing the able-bodied, but for rehabilitating the character of the dependent. Conventional wisdom explained poverty as a character weakness that forced labor would remedy.[8] The first workhouse in Virginia was built in Fredericksville Parish of Louisa County in 1756, and others sprang up in various parts of the colony in 1767, 1771, and 1772.[9]

Until workhouses were built, the parish church cared for the poor; the vestrymen, usually the leading men of the community, levied and collected taxes from the tithable (white males sixteen years of age and older), investigated cases of indigence, and decided upon the amount and kind of assistance. Under this system, the poor received relief in the forms of supplies or assignment to the homes of friends or relatives for work and care, commonly called "outdoor relief." As workhouses became available, the poor were assigned to these institutions.[10]

The coming of the American Revolution created suspicion of all powers of the church and led to a complete overhaul of Virginia's welfare system. The church was relieved of its authority and responsibility for the poor and was replaced by the state, throwing the whole system of poor relief more completely into the realm of partisan politics. Acts of the Virginia Assembly in 1780 and 1785 dissolved the vestry system and established provisions for election of an overseer of the poor in each district of a county. The 1785 statute, which formed the basis of the welfare system until the twentieth century, gave county courts the authority to divide counties into districts and to hold elections of "freeholders and householders only," for the election of "overseers of the poor." The overseers would have powers formerly held by vestrymen and would also appoint a superintendent of the workhouse.[11] In Louisa County by the time of the Reconstruction period (1865–69), overseers of the poor decided who would receive assistance in the form of food and supplies—"outside relief"—and who should be placed in the workhouse. Those impoverished by temporary illness commonly received outside relief in their homes.

Ideally, the workhouse was to be located on a farm under the supervision of a superintendent, usually a farmer. For his services, the superintendent got a salary, a house and board, and any proceeds from the sale of produce grown on the farm surrounding the workhouse. The demands upon the superintendent and his family were great, as the following job description shows. It appeared in the Louisa County Board of Supervisors' journal in 1898, when Louisa needed to find another superintendent.

> Qualifications for the incoming Overseer of the Poor by the Board of Supervisors. Sobriety, honesty, industry, and a faithful discharge of all his duties as laid down by laws and indicated by the Board. Close attention to his business, working as a hand on the farm, and as far as possible, keeping up repairs with his own mechanical skill, keeping always in view the health and comfort of the paupers, also paying attention to their conduct, compelling decency and good behavior but conducting the whole business with due regard to economy. His wife shall be neat, clearly and always on the alert to keep the paupers clean and comfortable, keeping bedsteads and bedding clean and free from vermin, seeing that their food is properly cooked and served, and working under all circumstances to keep the premises in a neat and sightly condition.[12]

Few superintendents could meet these exacting requirements and those who served found little time for carefully administering their "business." No records were maintained to show the reason for a person's admission, and many lived and died in the "almshouse" or "poorhouse," as they came to be called, with no record of their lives except date of admission and discharge, sometimes by death. Often their names were unknown.[13]

Almshouses failed, however, primarily because they were required to house and care for cases for which they were neither intended nor equipped. Since they were the only institutions of public welfare, gradually they became a collection point for a variety of abandoned people: the tubercular, blind, epileptic, infirm, emotionally ill. Generally, those suffering from handicaps and incapacitating ills of all kinds soon filled the almshouses, and few knew of the actual conditions in which they lived. One of the reasons these dens of inhumanity went unnoticed was their often remote location. A State Board of Charities and Corrections inspected almshouses in 1908 and noted that one of the general and unfortunate aspects of these institutions was their remoteness, often so far from settled areas that they were seldom visited. In fact, the greater expense of the board in its investigation was "team hire" to reach the almshouse from the nearest railroad station.[14]

Neither of the two solutions to poverty, then, which local communities like Louisa had inherited, the almshouse and outdoor relief, had proven satisfactory by 1865. The almshouse had drifted far from its first vision as a remedy to poverty and had become a custodial institution.[15] Outdoor relief had never been popular. Indeed, the workhouse had been established to reduce the need for outdoor relief. Moreover, it was unpopular because it did not provide the same opportunity for rehabilitation many assumed the almshouse did. Public outdoor relief was supposed to be a temporary dole of material aid—a little food, fuel, or clothing—not a long-term program, lest the individual become "dependent" upon outside assistance.[16]

Thus, in 1865 when southern counties were faced with 4 million unemployed freedmen and countless poor whites, a welfare problem of staggering dimensions, public officials had little in the way of past wisdom upon which they might borrow. Nor were these the only problems after the war. Welfare needs had to compete with those of repairing war damage, financing a newly instituted public school system, building roads, attacking epidemics of disease, and covering ordinary administrative expenses involved in county government, such as paying the salaries of public officials, registering voters, certifying elections, and maintaining records. During Virginia's Reconstruction era, local governments tried to shirk their responsibilities to the poor and attempted to squeeze welfare funds out of the federal government, specifically the Freedmen's Bureau. It was a period marked by disputes between local and federal officials over responsibility for the poor.

THE LOUISA POOR DURING RECONSTRUCTION

The Freedmen's Bureau had been established primarily to aid and protect freed slaves. In many counties, however, the bureau also issued rations to poor whites, at least for a brief period. Bureau officers were aware that many poor whites (as well as poor blacks) were refusing the ignominious solution of the poorhouse. The bureau officer in Goochland County, Louisa's neighbor, commented that many of the poor would suffer a great deal rather than go to the poorhouse.[17] Poor whites, who saw in the bureau a way to avoid the poorhouse, and county officials, who hoped for federal help in dealing with poverty, must have been disappointed in September 1865 when a general order was issued, declaring that destitute whites would no longer come within the provision of the bureau.[18]

As far as the freedmen were concerned, the bureau's policy was to encourage each county to care for them, either by placing them in the poorhouse or by providing some form of outdoor relief. If this failed, the bureau promised to fill the gap by issuing rations itself. In the cases where local officials could not be induced to aid freedmen, the bureau still hesitated to grant them rations of food and clothing and did so only as a last resort. Typically, as noted in Chapter II, Freedmen's Bureau officials concentrated on getting laborers to sign labor contracts with local landlords. An order of the district superintendent in July 1865 directed field officers not to issue rations to anyone able to work so long as employment could be found.[19] In fact, the principles to be adhered to in regard to paupers was to get each county, parish, township, or city to care and provide for its own poor.[20]

When asked by the Freedmen's Bureau about the kind of assistance they were providing the poor, local officials argued they were doing all they could or made excuses for why they could not do more. Orange County overseers of the poor responded to the bureau's inquiry about what they intended to do with destitute freedmen by asserting they had neither the authority nor the ability to care for these individuals. The Board of Supervisors, they argued, could support people only in the poorhouse and that was presently filled with poor whites. Moreover, the present levy for such support did not include blacks, who therefore could not receive aid from these funds. Fluvanna County reported that it gave out rations "in extreme cases" and as a rule "helped those who cannot help themselves." Culpeper County asserted that county funds would be distributed to poor blacks and whites indiscriminately, but that funds in general were short because not enough had been appropriated to take care of the poor; the white poor would receive priority. Giles County assured the bureau that all freedmen who had been residents of the county for twelve months and "who are not able to take care of themselves" would be provided assistance. Those moving to the county who could not support themselves would be "run out." Other counties hid behind legal barriers whenever they could. Princess Anne reminded the bureau that Sections 7 and 8, Chapter 51, of the Code of Virginia forbade any county from taking care of whites or blacks coming into the county from another county. The most astounding report came from Essex County, whose funds were limited because their poor funds had been invested in various bank and railroad stocks, none of which were now paying a dividend.[21]

The Freedmen's Bureau elicited these responses from individual counties by sending a questionnaire to the chairmen of county boards of overseers. It asked four questions: Will you give the same aid to destitute blacks settled in your county as whites? What will be the extent and character of this aid? How will the aid be granted? Will you provide for all destitute freedmen, and if not, what proportion? Louisa County responded much the way other counties did. In answer to the first question, the overseers claimed they would give aid to destitute blacks as soon as the money was raised by a general levy. They promised that the extent and character of the aid would be the same as that given to poor whites. To the question of how the aid would be granted, overseers stated, "Many years ago houses and lands were set aside by the county where those in need of county support are sent." They promised that as many as possible would be cared for there. Louisa officials said nothing about providing rations to those outside the poorhouse. Finally, they assured the bureau that freedmen would be treated like white persons, without discrimination.[22] In the final reports to the bureau concerning the poor, Louisa officials claimed that all indigent whites were being cared for by civil authorities, and that freedmen were being placed in the poorhouse if necessary.[23] Did Louisa do as much for its poor as promised in these reports? How did local governments respond to poverty? How much assistance did they provide? Could Louisa have done more to alleviate poverty, or were potential sources of revenue too overburdened to provide further relief? These questions are best answered by focusing upon the county in the period after Reconstruction when the Freedmen's Bureau had dissolved and the poor had become the sole responsibility of the county government. An examination of the county budget and local tax records of representative Louisans will show where promise and fulfillment began and ended.

POOR RELIEF 1870–1900

In 1870 Louisa County approved expenditures of $1,150 for rations of food and clothing furnished to paupers outside the poorhouse. The superintendent of the poorhouse was paid $100 in salary and allowed an additional $150 for expenses. Other expenses related to the alleviation of poverty included $27 for building expenses, $7 for a blacksmith, and $328 in sundry items, all of which was spent at the poorhouse. A physician was hired specifically for residents and paid $50. Eight coffins were furnished to bury the destitute during the year, at a cost of $16. Thus, a total of $1,828 was spent on various aspects of poverty in 1870. This figure represented 25.8 percent of the total county revenues of $7,081 collected in that year.[24]

Throughout this period, the county provided assistance to the poor in the form of coffins for those who died in poverty. Typically, county officials sought out local farm laborers, who were paid $1 to $2 to build a coffin. Their names indicated many hired for this sobering task were black laborers, such as Andrew Carter or Peter Homes, two hands of Thomas Watson.

It is impossible to tell how much each pauper actually received or how many were aided. Of the above amount, a maximum of $1,478 ($1,150 in outside aid and $328 spent on the poor at the poorhouse) might have gone to the poor themselves, but did it? Local records indicate payment not to the individual poor, but to storekeepers, the sheriff, members of the Board of Supervisors, and other intermediaries, who presented claims for supplying poor families. It is impossible to tell how much of this food and clothing ever reached the poor.

In 1878 the Board of Supervisors established guidelines for outdoor aid, which was not to exceed $1.50 per family per month and preferably to range between 50¢ and $1.00.[25] If we use the figure of $1.00 as a measure for 1870 and assume 1,478 householders were aided during the year, the county could have been supporting only a maximum of 123 families per month, a figure far below the 5,000–7,000 destitute freedmen the Louisa Freedmen's Bureau officer had estimated to be in need of assistance after the war.[26] Moreover, a dollar per month scarcely guaranteed anything but starvation.

In subsequent years, the county aided the poor at levels comparable to these figures for 1870. In 1885 outside aid was higher, totaling $1,835, but still about 25 percent of county revenues for that year. Twenty-seven coffins were supplied to bury the dead.[27] Expenditures for the poor peaked in 1890–91, during the midst of a harsh depression, when the county spent 29 percent of its budget ($2,007) on poverty and supplied 56 coffins for the poor. By 1900–1901 outside aid was down to $981, the lowest amount since 1870.[28]

Over the years it became more and more difficult for paupers to receive aid, and the amount each person could be given was reduced. In 1879 the Board of Supervisors ordered allowances to paupers outside the poorhouse to be reduced by one-third to one-half of previous amounts, and in 1880 the maximum allowance per family per month was lowered to 75¢, "except in exceptional cases and less when adequate." In 1895 the supervisors established a ceiling of $1,200 for all outside rations.[29] Each overseer of the poor was directed to file a list of all persons in his district furnished with supplies, giving names and monthly allowance.[30] In 1887 the instructions became even more specific.

> The supervisor of each district is hereby ordered to appoint one discreet and reliable person in his district who, after procurring from the overseer of the poor a complete list, showing the monthly allowances to each, of all the paupers living in the district who receives outside help, shall be charged with the duty of visiting each person on the poor list of the district to ascertain their precise condition as follows: age, physical condition and health, extent of help that might be available from other sources, property owned, and any other information helpful to the Board in determining the propriety of making an allowance.[31]

County officials also watched like hawks the amounts spent at the almshouse. When A. B. Poindexter was chosen superintendent of the almshouse in 1875, a post he held for fifteen years, he was chosen "because of his economy, faithfulness, and ability . . ." and praised in 1879 for spending only $759 of the $1,000 allotted to him. In the same year his salary was raised to $150 per year because of his success in holding down expenses, and in 1888 it was raised again to $200.[32] In those years for which records existed, the almshouse had an average of twenty-four persons per year in residence, and the records indicate none of them could work.[33]

Throughout the period from 1870 to 1900, the percentage of the county budget devoted to welfare typically hovered around one-fourth of total disbursements. Yet, as noted above, the poor themselves got less and less aid. Rising administrative costs explain this strange combination of circumstances. The superintendent at the almshouse received two raises in salary, part of the increase in administrative overhead. In 1875 four overseers of the poor were elected, and three were given annual salaries of $20 and the fourth $30 for these positions, which continued throughout the period of study. In 1887, when the overseers were required to produce lists of the poor in their districts, they were paid $10 each for producing the lists, and the same lists were compiled during the next four years. Other expenses included repairs to the poorhouse and the hiring of a physician to inoculate the poor at the poorhouse during several smallpox epidemics.[34] Thus, the reductions in direct relief to the poor were offset by increased amounts spent on indirect administrative expenses, and generally the county spent the same amount for poverty while the poor themselves received ever diminishing amounts.

In 1900 outdoor relief was virtually ended in Louisa, with the following justification:

> In view of the fact that outside pauper aid had become an unnecessary and useless burden to the taxpayer, and in view of the fact also that this question has gotten beyond the control of the Board, it is agreed that after September 1, 1900 no aid will be extended to the poor of Louisa County outside the county poorhouse unless every applicant for such aid shall come before the Board assembled in regular session on August 25, 1900 and in person or thro [sic] their representative show their cause, which must be approved by the whole Board why the county should be thus burdened.[35]

In other words, Louisa's political leadership felt secure enough by 1900 to eliminate most assistance to the poor, except the poorhouse itself, which always represented the smallest portion of the cost.

Poverty had not been eliminated, of course. The leadership was merely serving notice that the poor could expect far less in the future than they had received in the past. Per capita, assistance had steadily declined since Reconstruction. It had also become harder to qualify for relief.

More importantly, poor relief had become another part of the surplus-extraction structure. Relief policies increasingly served the interests of the nonpoor. Overall expenditures for poor relief actually increased in the form of payments to doctors, overseers, superintendents, district supervisors, and other "servants" of the poor. Tax policies followed a similar course.

TAXATION AND THE POOR

The question of Louisa's response to poverty has been answered, but could the county have done more? It could be argued that the expenditure of one-fourth of county revenues for poverty was indicative of a rather generous response. Besides disbursements for salaries in 1899, for example, which composed 47 percent of all county disbursements, poverty was the next-greatest expense (26 percent).[36] These figures, however, give no indication of the potential of the county to provide more extensive benefits. Louisans of the nineteenth century complained of high taxes just as loudly as do Americans of the twentieth century, but was their complaining a strategy calculated to keep taxes low or an indication of overbearing demands? The diminished wealth of the postwar South seems to lend even greater credence to the claim that nineteenth-century southerners were overtaxed, but really how great was the burden of taxation?

These questions are best answered by examining the records of wealth and taxation of Louisa farmers who represent different economic groups (Table 5.1). Thomas Watson and Robert A. Duncan represent the wealthy planter class, who accumulated sizable estates before the war and ranked in the top 5 percent of the population in terms of wealth after the war. Winston Arnett and Abner Foster represent the poor tenant class, whose accumulations of real and personal property placed them among the county's poor. In each case, the total value of all land, buildings, and personal property is given and the total taxes paid for the sample years 1863, 1870, and 1890. The tax rate is the total tax divided by total worth.[37]

Table 5.1 The Taxation of Selected Farmers, Louisa County, 1863, 1870, and 1890

	1863			1870			1890		
	Total Value ($)	Total Tax ($)	Tax Rate (%)	Total Value ($)	Total Tax ($)	Tax Rate (%)	Total Value ($)	Total Tax ($)	Tax Rate (%)
Thomas Watson (White planter)	34,099	333.00	1	31,446	158.23	.5	25,829	196.42	.8
Robert Duncan (White planter)	41,081	412.82	1	17,973	91.00	.5			
Winston Arnett (Black tenant)	not located			80	1.40	2	70	1.51	2
Abner Foster (White tenant)	not located			45	1.23	3	50	1.37	2.7

Source: Land and Personal Property Taxbook, Louisa County, 1863, 1870, and 1890.

Not on landbook, but personal property rate was .15

Tax revenue was sharply reduced from the levels of the slave period.[38] However, the county's diminished income was not solely the result of the loss of slave revenues. Table 5.1 shows that Thomas Watson and Robert A. Duncan, two former slaveowning planters, were paying taxes at the rate of 1 percent of their total worth in 1863. In 1870 these same two Louisans paid taxes at a rate one-half of that of 1863. Watson's estate was valued at about $34,000 in 1863 and $31,500 in 1870, a reduction of about 8 percent in total worth, while his tax bill in the two periods dropped from $333 to $158, a reduction of 52 percent. In other words, greater revenues for county needs could have been produced simply by taxing at wartime rates.

Even more striking, however, and of far greater significance, is the unfair if not fraudulent way in which the tax burden was distributed. The wealthy were not only paying one-half of what they had paid during slavery, they were also paying proportionately much less than the poor after the war. Winston Arnett and Abner Foster, two Louisa tenants with property worth less than $100, paid taxes in 1870 which constituted 2 to 3 percent of their total worth. The poor were paying taxes at a rate four to six times that of the rich! Clearly, the unlanded were bearing the greater burden of taxation. These figures reveal no conclusive evidence of racial distinction (except that the white tenant paid at a slightly higher tax rate than the black tenant for reasons that are unclear) but rather compelling evidence of class preferences. Moreover, the tenants, in terms of their holdings, represented a substantial majority of the Louisa population. For example, among the sample of farmers, those who paid a personal property tax of $2 or less in 1880 (i.e., held property worth less than $100) composed 59 percent of the white and 99 percent of the black population.[39] Obviously, Louisa could have generated more revenue than it did. This would not have required "soaking the rich"; just treating them like the poor would have been enough.

THOSE WHO GOVERNED

Taxing the poor at one rate and the wealthy at another was not the only way that political patronage reinforced class dominance. The social origin of Louisa's leadership and their persistent rotation among the available county positions served the same end.

Dr. P. P. May was chairman of the Board of Supervisors in 1876, a county physician, and owner of 1,153 acres of land and farm buildings worth $8,551, placing him in the top 5 percent of the county's economic elite. In 1863 he held forty slaves worth $15,000, large herds of cattle, sheep, and hogs, and $12,000 in bonds, a total wealth in personal property of $40,345. After the war he combined the roles of physician, farmer, and politician, serving on the Board of Supervisors for at least fourteen years. Matthew A. Anderson, another member of the board in 1876, had been a large slaveholder in 1863 (twenty slaves) and a large landowner after the war (413 acres) and served on the board for six years (1870–78) before becoming postmaster in 1893. Henry W. Murray, another supervisor in 1876, owned nine slaves in 1863 (worth $5,200), owned personal property valued at $8,655, and also practiced law. After the war he sold most of his estate, purchased a valuable half-acre near the courthouse, and served repeated terms on the Board of Supervisors. Only H. J. Wale among the supervisors of 1876 could not be located on the 1863 personal property taxbook, although he owned a large farm in 1876 (436 acres) and also served as a postmaster after repeated terms on the board. Numerous other county officials in positions of leadership in 1876 were former slaveowners, including six of nine justices of the peace, the superintendent of schools (also a minister as well as a prewar slaveholder), two of six city councilmen, the treasurer, the clerk of court, the commonwealth's attorney, and one of the two commissioners of revenue. Nearly 50 percent of the county officials (16 of 33) in 1876 had been slaveholders and 85 percent were landowners.[40] Clearly, property holding was an important path to leadership, and landowners together with physicians, ministers, dentists, lawyers, or combinations of these, dominated county government.

These biographies justify calling the local leaders a "ring" or "courthouse clique"; the same individuals circulated among the available positions. The explanation for such an apparently undemocratic polity lies in the organizational makeup of the Democratic party, which dominated state and local government after Reconstruction.

Democrats, or "Conservatives," as they were called, revised the "Underwood constitution," drafted during Reconstruction; the changes allowed county government to be controlled by a smaller group of men. The Underwood Constitution, named after the hated carpetbagger Judge John C. Underwood who presided over the convention in 1868–69, divided counties into townships, each headed by a supervisor. The supervisors were elected each year along with a clerk, assessor, collector of revenue, commissioner of the roads, overseer of the poor, three justices of the peace, and three constables. Planters disliked this system, especially in counties with black majorities, where the black vote threatened white rule. Between 1872 and 1875 Conservatives controlled the General Assembly and drastically altered the Reconstruction constitution. They abolished the offices of township clerk, assessor, collector, and road commissioner, two of three constables; divided counties into magisterial districts, each headed by an elected supervisor; made the overseer of the poor and surveyor appointive positions; and changed the time of local elections from November to May to avert federal intervention. The amendments also provided for a county court composed of a salaried judge appointed by the General Assembly for a six-year term.[41] The changes abolished four offices, consolidating police powers under one official, administrative powers under the Board of Supervisors, and judicial powers under a state-appointed judge.

In 1884, county government became even more undemocratic. As a result of the Anderson-McCormick Election Law, the General Assembly selected a local chairman of the Democratic party and controlled local government through this official. He selected a local electoral board who chose election judges and clerks from every precinct whose names were submitted to the General Assembly for approval. At least one of three judges and clerks was supposed to be from the opposition party. Usually, this was a renegade Republican or Negro.[42]

A final technique guaranteed control of the courthouse clique. The change from the township to the magisterial district system permitted the redrawing of precinct lines. In Louisa they were drawn in such a way as to nullify the black vote. In three county districts—Green Springs, Cuckoo, and Jackson—precincts were organized with white majorities in 1888. Green Springs had three of six precincts with more whites registered than blacks, Cuckoo had two of four, and in Jackson the lines had been drawn to give whites a majority in each precinct.[43] Moreover, the registration figures for 1888 showed more whites registered to vote than the number of white males twenty-one years of age and over on the 1888 personal property taxbook.[44]

Thus, long before the disfranchising constitution of 1902, the black vote had been nullified in Louisa. And, it should come as no surprise that Louisa remained in the political control of a small band of party faithful.

Nor should it be surprising that the leadership dispensed a great amount of patronage upon itself and other powerful economic members of the community through the county treasury. The journal of the Board of Supervisors year after year recorded payments to these leaders or other landowners, like Thomas S. Watson, Dr. Matthew Pendleton, Matthew A. Hope, or Henry W. Murray, for "dividing the county into townships," "carrying returns to the clerk's office," or serving as temporary surveyors, road supervisors, or commissioners of elections. Other opportunities included taking paupers to the poorhouse and numerous small tasks. Thus, the remaining three-fourths of the disbursements not spent on poverty was largely spent on leaders' salaries and claims presented by them for services rendered to the county.[45]

Some insight into the way patronage politics worked may be gained by observing the response to smallpox epidemics. In 1882 the county was faced with the need to borrow money to buy vaccine and pay physicians to vaccinate the victims. It borrowed $2,000 from six wealthy landowners of the county, some of whom may have been related to the members of the Board of Supervisors. Dr. R. Basset, a local physician-planter, was hired and paid $7 a day for 84 days' work, or $588. He later presented an additional bill for $50 for "helpers." In 1894 when the epidemic returned, Dr. Pendleton, a former member of the board, was hired to vaccinate county residents and paid $7 per day, and again in 1902.[46] The point is not that the county erred in borrowing from its own residents, providing these services, or even hiring family members, but that the county treasury had been transformed into a tool of patronage largely serving a small elite while others in the county suffered daily the pangs of starvation and want.

Some of the human costs of such a system can be glimpsed in the statistics. Between 1888 and 1901 Louisa furnished an average of twenty-four coffins each year to bury the pauper dead.[47] In other words, each month two Louisans died who were too poor to pay for their own burial.

Such were the ways in which politics became part of the surplus-extraction structure. Poor relief gradually evolved into a source of income for local patrons. It was largely supported by taxes assessed upon the poor themselves, who paid much more than their fair share of taxes. The tax dollars that were not redistributed to the wealthy in the form of fees for services rendered to the poor were redistributed to them for a host of other services associated with county government. Poverty was not alleviated by such a system, it was guaranteed by it. Faced with an economic system that confined them to a class of dependent laborers and a political system that offered little or no relief, Louisa's poor ultimately dealt with poverty within their own households.

VI

.

Households and Families

Limited opportunities outside of agriculture,[1] low returns or wage rates within agriculture, large families, and public assistance held to 75¢ per family per month or the almshouse exerted great pressures on Louisa families who refused to migrate. Moreover, the kinds of social welfare programs familiar to the twentieth century were absent. Nothing like workmen's compensation existed to soften the blows of accidents; no unemployment insurance cushioned the impact of depression; no social security aided those beyond the years of productive work; and no life insurance provided for burial expenses. Even the self-help institutions that sprang up in urban areas to aid the indigent were nearly (though not totally) absent in Louisa.[2] Without outside assistance, accidents, sickness, loss of job, aging, or death became critical events in the lives of the poor.

As the shadow of poverty crossed the thresholds of Louisa's poor, families attempted to soften its blows.[3] This chapter analyzes the impact of poverty upon the family and household by looking at the composition of individual households of the sample population during various stages of their development and under different economic circumstances.

HOUSEHOLD COMPOSITION

Table 6.1 summarizes the results of a sorting of the "farmer" sample population of Louisa county into family types, which were determined on the basis of the persons actually residing in the

This chapter is based on an earlier version that appeared in Shifflett, "The Household Composition of Rural Black Families: Louisa County, Virginia, 1880," *Journal of Interdisciplinary History* 6, no. 2 (Autumn 1975): 235–60; by permission of *The Journal of Interdisciplinary History* and The M.I.T. Press, Cambridge, Massachusetts.

household at the time of the 1880 census.[4] Among both racial groups, the simple nuclear family was the dominant form of family organization; nearly half of all the households in 1880 were of this kind. In spite of the attention given to the woman-headed household in the literature on the black family, the male-absent household was relatively unimportant in Louisa County.[5] If the nuclear family is a measure of stability, then Louisa's families were decidedly stable in the Emancipation era.[6]

Table 6.1 Household Composition of Families of the Same Population, Louisa County, 1880

Family Type	% of Families		Number	
	Black	White	Black	White
Simple nuclear family (husband and wife with or without unmarried children)	46	47	116	136
Supplemented nuclear family (simple nuclear family with relatives in the household)	18	13	44	37
Augmented nuclear family (simple nuclear family with outsiders in the household)	8	14	20	41
All other	28	26	71	74

Source: Ms Census of Population, Louisa County, 1880.

More importantly, over half of the families lived in domestic groups of another form. The major categories were core nuclear families with relatives (supplemented nuclear) or unrelated members (augmented nuclear), which together composed over a fourth of all black and white families in the sample. Thus, a substantial number of Louisa families in 1880 lived in residentially extended households composed of others besides the core nuclear family.

THE FAMILY LIFE CYCLE

The cross-sectional view, however, disguises as much as it reveals.

It is a snapshot of family life at one moment, not a motion picture of the family and its internal changes over a lifetime. In order to represent the family as a dynamic institution with its own age and life cycle, I have grouped the households of the sample population of Louisa County on the basis of certain criteria. The resulting groups are four: *newlyweds* (newly married couples without children); *young families* (couples where the wife was less than forty-five years of age with children in the family, but where no children were employed or married); *mid-stage families* (couples where the wife was of any age but where children were employed, married, or both); and *mature families* (couples where the wife was more than forty-five years of age and where all children had left home).[7]

When Louisa families were distributed on the basis of this model, it became obvious that family types varied with stage of development. Table 6.2 shows that in the sample population of Louisa County, black families most often took nuclear form at two stages, when children began to arrive (young families) and later when children began to leave their families or origin for employment and marriage (mid-stage). White families also had higher percentages of simple nuclear families in some stages than in others. The simple nuclear family was least likely in the households of black newlyweds. At this stage of the family life cycle, 90 percent of black families included relatives or outsiders. Frequently, white families at this stage also had relatives and outsiders resident (46 percent). The white family, however, at the time of formation was not nearly so prone to take in these groups as was the black family.

By tracing two families through the federal censuses for the period from 1870 to 1900, we can see clearly the actual changes in household composition common to large numbers of Louisa families.

John Shelton, a twenty-year-old black agricultural laborer, lived in a household in 1870 composed of himself, his sixteen-year-old wife, Isabella, and a baby less than one year old. By 1880 there were more children: two daughters, born in 1873 and 1879, respectively, and one son, born in 1874. However, Shelton's was no longer a simple nuclear family; it now contained his fifty-year-old mother-in-law and his nineteen-year-old sister-in-law. By 1900 his household had changed again to include, besides John and Isabella, six children, one of whom was his married daughter, with her child, whose father was absent. During a span of thirty years the Shelton household had changed from a simple nuclear family to a supplemented nuclear family and, finally, to a type which was placed in the category "all other." Changes may also have occurred in other years.

Table 6.2　Family Type by Stage of Development
Sample Population, Louisa County, 1880

	FamilyType			
	Supplemented		Augmented	
Stage of Development	Nuclear	Nuclear	Nuclear	(N)
		(percentages)		
Newlyweds				
White	54	31[a]	15	(13)
Black	10	60	30	(10)
Young families				
White	59[a]	19	22[a]	(104)
Black	67	22	11	(79)
Mid-stage families				
White	67[a]	14	20[a]	(66)
Black	73	17	10	(70)
Matured families				
White	65[a]	13[a]	23	(31)
Black	46	36	18	(22)

Source: Ms Census of Population, Louisa County, 1880.

[a]Black-white differences significant at 0.10. Tests of statistical significance were made on this table and others below to determine the probability of differences in sample findings among the two groups from those of the population universe that were attributable to sampling error. At the 0.90 level (one = tail P = 0.10), differences in question could not be accounted for on the grounds of sampling error and thus the sample differences reflect real differences in the population universe. For an explanation of this procedure and the tables used for the tests, see Gerhard E. Lenski, *The Religious Factor: A Sociological Study of Religion's Impact on Politics, Economics, and Family Life* (New York: Greenwood, 1977), App. I, pp. 367–76. For further elaboration of these techniques, see Appendix, below.

David R. Hill, a twenty-five-year-old white agricultural laborer in 1870, lived in a household comprising his thirty-five-year-old wife, Eugina, two stepchildren, and several unrelated white residents. By 1880 they had acquired a farm of their own and his household now included his wife and her two children by a former marriage, plus two more children of his own: a daughter born in 1875 and a son born in 1877. By 1900 Hill's household included, besides Eugina, two sons, one of whom was employed as a postmaster and the other as a laborer, and a grandchild of one of his married children who was not residing in the house. During the thirty-year span, his household had changed from an augmented nuclear family to a simple nuclear family and then to a type not categorized in this chapter.

Clearly, the frequency of family types like nuclear or extended reveals little about family structure. A high percentage of nuclear families in a population merely reflects the demographic reality that in most societies the nuclear family type is the majority.[8] But, obviously, Louisa families were in constant flux, as relatives and unrelated persons moved in and out and their arrivals and departures altered household composition as the family cycle progressed. The larger issue is the question about the reasons for these changes. Were they related to cultural norms or did social and economic conditions affect household composition?

HOUSEHOLD AND ECONOMY

Hypothetically, it seems reasonable to assume that household composition at a given stage of the family cycle is neither wholly a product of cultural mores nor totally determined by economics. Yet, domestic groups must be able to survive as economic units before they can fulfill any of their social functions, and it makes little sense to talk about family forms in cultural terms without first ascertaining the extent to which they have been influenced by economic pressures. Indeed, it is not necessary to appeal to cultural differences in explaining household composition so long as social and economic factors provide a satisfactory answer. By assessing families' composition in the various phases of development in the light of their economic needs at each stage, the relationship between household composition and the social and economic order can be ascertained.

In Table 6.3 the sample population of Louisa County in 1880 is distributed according to the number of workers in the household supporting each consumer, or what shall be called the "consumer / worker ratio."[9] When this ratio was correlated with the family cycle, a graphic picture of the different burdens borne by Louisa families at various stages of their development emerged. For example, young families of both races had a high consumer / worker ratio; as children began to work, the ratio diminished.

Variations in the consumer / worker ratio can be illustrated by reference to the two households previously used as examples. Hill, the white agricultural laborer, had a ratio of 1.50 in 1870. By 1880, with the arrival of additional children, it rose to 6.00 and then declined to 1.67 in 1900 as his children found employment and began to leave home. The household of Shelton, the black agricultural laborer, initially had a consumer / worker ratio of 3.00 This was reduced to 1.75 in 1880 with the arrival of a working sister-in-law and with children now old enough to work. In 1900 the ratio returned to a level of 3.00. Changes in this ratio in these families confirm the hypothesis that labor needs varied over the family life cycle.

Table 6.3 Consumer/Worker Ratio by
Stage of Family Development,
Sample Population, Louisa County, 1880

	Consumer/Worker Ratio						
Stage of Development	1.00- 1.80	1.81- 2.33	2.34- 3.00	3.01- 5.00	5.01- 9.99	Over 10.00	(N)
			(percentage)				
Newlyweds							
Black	25	8	17	33	17	-	(12)
White	15	46	31	8	-	1	(13)
Young families							
Black	3	8	20	23	39	9	(82)
White	6	11	21	28	26	8	(107)
Mid-stage families							
Black	27	33	20	18	2	-	(94)
White	37	23	23	15	3	-	(71)
Mature families							
Black	9	24	30	30	3	3	(33)
White	16	32	21	18	11	3	(38)

Source: Ms Census of Population, Louisa County, 1880.

Newlywed and mature families, however, exhibited less uniform patterns than those of young and mid-stage families, especially in the case of black families. Two-thirds of these young and old black households had ratios above 2.33, whereas only one-third of young white households fell in this range, and half of older households did so. It is also evident in the home of Shelton, where the ratio at these two stages is higher than might be expected.

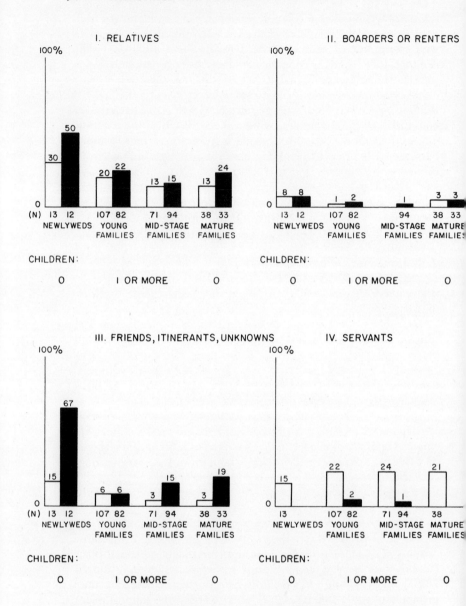

Figure 6.1. Household Residents over the Family Cycle. (Prepared by the graphics department of Virginia Polytechnic Institute and State University.)

Consumer / worker ratios above 2.33 in households where children were not resident and where household economic pressures
were more relaxed indicated that families periodically contained
residents other than the core nuclear family. Who actually resided in
these households, during what stage of the family cycle, and why?

Figure 6.1 shows household composition at the various stages of
the family cycle. Graph I gives the percentages of all black and white
households that contained relatives. Graphs II, III, and IV show the
kinds of outsiders present only in those households that contained
outsiders. For black newlyweds, the outsiders most commonly in
residence were friends, persons of unknown relationship, or itinerants. Boarders and renters in much lower percentages were the
other outsiders in these young households. When children arrived,
the number of friends, unknowns, or itinerants was sharply reduced,
as was the number of boarders, and a few households began to take
in servants. As children began to work and marry, friends returned
to these maturing households; few boarders and servants remained.
As the family's life cycle matured, servants disappeared completely,
the number of boarders increased slightly, and friends again made up
the largest group of outsiders in black households.

Black and white households also differed in the frequency with
which relatives were included. One out of three white households
began with some kind of relative resident, while half of black
newlyweds did so. Although the number of households with relatives declined from an initial high point, one-fourth of the black
households still had relatives in the mature stage.

Apparently, household composition among young and mid-stage
families was the result of increased pressures to produce more. As
children began to arrive and the burdens of support became heavier
on adult members of the household, families of both racial groups
changed to assure greater economic security. However, as the
figures also show, the response of the two communities was not the
same.

Among the black families, as economic burdens mounted with the
arrival of children (when the consumer / worker ratio increased
beyond 2.33), the number of consumers was reduced and black
families unburdened themselves of relatives and other outsiders.
During the mid-stage when children began to work and relieve adult
members of some of the responsibility of economic support, black
families were again able to take in outsiders such as friends. White
families also reacted to the same pressure to expand the volume of
economic activity and provide for the economic well-being of the

family. However, many of these families were able to exploit a readily available source of servant labor in 1880. Although white households did empty of a few friends and relatives, their labor needs in these two middle stages were supplied mostly by servants.

Hence, both black and white families during their youth and mid-career sought to reach a point of equilibrium, where the volume of household economic activity satisfied family demands, by continually altering household composition. Black families made different adjustments because of their incapacity to meet family demands otherwise. During these two stages internal economic factors provide satisfactory explanations of household composition. If, however, the volume of economic activity determines household composition throughout the life cycle, as predicted, then one would also have expected household economic factors to account for family residence decisions during the other two stages as well—newlyweds and mature families—and also expect certain conditions to hold. For example, families in those stages where economic pressures are much more relaxed because of the absence of children would not be expected to include outsiders, relatives, or servants (working adults), since there is no internal economic need to increase production. Thus, one would expect the simple nuclear family—the family type with fewest available adult workers—to appear most frequently at stages in the family when the expansion of economic activity is least necessary—among newlyweds and mature families.

In fact, internal economic needs do not adequately explain household composition during the two end phases of the family cycle. As seen in Figure 6.1, white newlyweds and mature families included servant laborers in the household (contributing members) in significant numbers, even when there was no pressing need for additional residents to work (when the consumer / worker ratio was between 1.00 and 2.33). Neither did black families in these stages act according to predictions. Black newlyweds gave homes to large numbers of friends, and half of these new families included relatives for other reasons than a need for a source of labor.

Because of these residence choices, the simple nuclear family—a type anticipated among newlyweds and mature families—actually showed up more often in the middle stages of the family cycle. As Table 6.4 shows, among white families the simple nuclear type predominated throughout the cycle of development. Nonetheless, the lowest frequency came at just those instances where the null hypothesis—that the volume of economic activity determines family composition—predicted its highest frequency. In the case of black families, the null hypothesis makes less sense, since black families in these stages lived in supplemented or augmented families even more often that did the white.

Table 6.4   Simple Nuclear Family as a Percentage of Total Families, by Stage of Development, Sample Population, Louisa County, 1880

Stage of Development	% of Total Families		Number	
	Black	White	Black	White
Newlyweds	8	54	12	13
Young families[a]	65	57	82	107
Mid-stage families[a]	54	65	94	71
Mature families[a]	30	53	53	38

Source: Ms Census of Population, Louisa County, 1880.

[a]Black-White differences significant at 0.10.

Therefore, household composition was not merely a reflection of families' labor requirements, and the problem remains of explaining household composition during the first and final phases of family development. The explanation is that particular domestic groupings in these stages resulted from the forces of class and caste in Louisa in the last quarter of the nineteenth century.

When an index of economic status based upon holdings of land, machinery, livestock, and draft animals is applied to the entire 1880 sample and correlated with stages of the family cycle, racial differences in the life cycle become apparent. The access of whites, in general, to these means of production made it possible for white families to accumulate some wealth over the family cycle (Table 6.5). As white families matured, they generally acquired more goods —not merely consumables, but resources that enhanced their capacity to succeed in rural society. Hence, they enjoyed gains in status that are reflected here in the shift of mid-stage and mature white families into the third and highest economic quartiles, and in the consequent decline of families with fewer or no resources among the maturing households.

The same was not true of black families, however. Some made gains as families matured, but those households never included more than a small fraction of the black community. What is even more revealing, more mature families composed the lower rungs of the economic ladder—just that phase of family development when the greatest accumulation of resources might be expected. Black families made the most significant economic gains during the mid-stage of their life cycle when children were working, but as Table 6.5 shows, these gains were only temporary. Indeed, many black families tended to skid as the family matured.

Table 6.5   Correlation of Economic Status with Stage of
Family Development,
Sample Population, Louisa County, 1880

Economic Status	Newlyweds		Young Families		Mid-stage Families		Mature Families	
	Black	White	Black	White	Black	White	Black	White
			(percentages)					
Lower Quartile	67	46	68	30	55	21	61	18
Second Quartile	33	23	29	28	39	30	33	13
Third Quartile	-	23	1	20	5	20	6	34
Upper Quartile	-	8	-	22	-	30	-	34
(N)	(12)	(13)	(82)	(107)	(94)	(71)	(33)	(38)

Source: Ms Census of Population, Land and Personal Property Taxbook, Louisa County, 1880.

Rural poverty, of course, was not merely a racial phenomenon. White families were well represented among the lower ranks of the community. Families of both racial groups with limited means of production—i.e., plows, harrows, draft animals, and arable land — lived in a threatening tug-of-war between life and death.

However, race limited black access to productive factors and intensified poverty in the black community.[10] When these limitations were combined with parsimony in public welfare expenditures, black families were faced with greater problems of care for those who could not care for themselves. These conditions, rather than the consumer / worker ratio, explain black household composition during the early and late stages of the family life cycle.

Since black newlyweds and mature families most frequently included outsiders and relatives in their households, as Figure 6.1 shows, and since these were the periods in the family cycle when black families were the poorest, as Table 6.5 shows, obviously their inclusion is not related to internal labor needs. Ony if these people had been contributing members of the household would their presence have made economic sense. Perhaps some of them were making an economic contribution. Yet, the striking fact is that only about half of the outsiders whom the young and old families accepted were actually employed—that is, were workers rather than consumers. In the case of relatives, manuscript census schedules also revealed that black households most often took in mothers or mothers-in-law, not potential contributors like brothers and sisters. Therefore, both newlyweds and mature families, although relatively free from the burdens of supporting children, often became care-takers of aged dependents and homeless outsiders.

Black household composition in the first and final phases of the cycle was largely the result of exogenous factors. Black families provided homes for the aged, the homeless, and the unemployed at points in the family's development when economic burdens were less intense. These people sought such homes because their care and welfare were bound up with family and friends, and because no alternative sources of employment, income, accommodation, protection, or social welfare were available. The burden of poverty induced black families to rely on kinship networks, to become their brothers' keepers.[11]

In comparison, many poor white families could act on the model of *homo economicus* because they were able to find work and even employ servants. The augmented nuclear family was well represented .in all phases of the white families' development (Table 6.4). Moreover, nearly as many poor white families employed servant labor after the war as those in the higher ranges of the economic status index. Census data indicate that white augmented households included employed outsiders 93 percent of the time ($N = 38$). In addition, among the supplemented nuclear families (families with relatives resident), the group of relatives most frequently accepted were those more likely to be contributors—sisters and sisters-in-law—than consumers.

MARRIAGES, BIRTHS, AND DEATHS

Besides declining prices of food, out-migration, and family assistance, other factors also prevented Louisa's poverty from exploding into a crisis of more staggering proportions. Population growth could have made the crisis far more intense. Population pressures, however, were not as great because of poverty's impact upon marriages, births, and deaths.

On the average, between 1865 and 1900 black males and females married at slightly younger ages than whites. In both cases, marriage ages were later than those of the twentieth century. The mean age at marriage for white males was 25.2 and 23 for black males and 23 and 21 for white and black females, respectively.[12] The earlier age at marriage for black women also explains the larger size of the black family. The families might have easily been larger had couples not tried to limit family size.[13]

Population pressures were also mitigated by limits on birth rates. Louisa marriages were not characterized by the immediate arrival of children. In a random sample of the 1900 population of Louisa, for those cases in which it could be determined,[14] spacing of children accomplished by couples in the two racial groups varied. In neither case, however, did children arrive immediately after marriage. Among whites, the mean interval was two years between marriage and the arrival of the first child. The interval was even longer in the black community, where on the average the first child did not arrive until three years after marriage. The mean interval between the first and second child was nearly two years for both groups, while succeeding arrivals evidence only slight differences. In no case was the interval ever less than two years for either group. Delayed marriage was also accompanied by a regular spacing of children; the popular notion that poor rural black and white families had one child after another does not describe the case in the economically marginal economy of Louisa. Rather, children arrived at predictable intervals in spite of the absence of modern forms of birth control. Whether the spacing was the result of nineteenth-century practices of birth control, such as interruption of the sexual act, or of the lowered chances of conception among lactating mothers, or merely a result of poor nutrition could not be determined.

The grimmest damper on population expansion was death. Surprisingly, Louisa County registered deaths by age and cause for a brief period between 1864 and 1870. Unfortunately, this valuable record must have been maintained carelessly because the numbers of recorded deaths in all of those years totaled only 699, while in 1880 federal census noted 350 deaths for that year alone. Since the 1880 census appeared to be a much more accurate record of deaths, death rates are based upon this record. High infant mortality characterized black males in 1880, when infant deaths were 34 percent greater for black males than for the population as a whole.[15] The black male infant mortality rate was 211.1 per thousand, compared with 165.8 for black females, the next highest rate, and far above the 113.4 and 101 reported for white males and females, respectively.[16] In both cases, infant mortality took a terrific toll of the population. Black females also recorded high death rates. In the age group 19–24, they had 43 percent more deaths than the general population and 62 percent more deaths in the age group 25–34.[17] Black males, however, recorded greater numbers of deaths in higher age categories, although not as great as white males and females. Female deaths among whites also outstripped males, although at later ages than was the case among the black population. Females of both races had a shorter life expectancy than males.[18]

Furthermore, marriage data on widows and widowers suggests the greater longevity of Louisa males. The marriage registers between 1859 and 1901 recorded nearly four times as many remarrying widowers as widows.[19] Thus, males of both racial groups often witnessed the earlier deaths of their wives, unlike the more common experience of the twentieth century, in which male life expectancy is typically below that of females.

Poverty often necessitated work outside the home, but the shorter life spans of women was due to a combination of circumstances.[20] Overwork alone would not have shortened their life span, but overwork coupled with the debilitating effects of bearing larger numbers of children than modern women meant that rural women of the nineteenth century had very harsh lives. The censuses of 1870 and 1900 indicate the average family size in Louisa County for the four decades was 5.5.[21] This figure, however, includes women who never married or never produced children and therefore underestimates the average number of children each mother actually bore. In addition, this average is also distorting because it is based upon living children and does not reflect the numbers of children ever borne by the mother. Other evidence more nearly reveals the extent of childbearing. Of those white mothers who had children, the average number ever borne was 4.9, and for black mothers the average number of children ever borne was 6.2.[22] Thus, more frequent childbirth and the women's need to work to support the family could explain the excess of males in the higher age groups, if the hardship led to premature deaths among black and white women.

THE DEMOGRAPHY OF POVERTY

High infant and child mortality, delayed marriages, definite spacing of children, early deaths of working women, shifting household composition, and the caretaking role of the family, all underscore the personal meaning of indigence. Decisions about marriage, family size, arrival of children, even about where to call home, were not merely normative issues but hard economic questions. And they were scarcely decisions at all, in the sense that the word implies a real choice. For the poor, life was simple. Most things had already been decided by the same fate that had marked out some for poverty, others wealth. Life was a matter of "keeping on, keeping on." They understood its hopelessness and kept on. Therein lies their heroism.

VII

·

Conclusion:
The Roots of Poverty in Louisa County

Louisa was a functioning social system where man and land came together in an essential and timeless relationship, first as master and slave, then as lord and tenant. The nature of this elementary relationship holds the key to Louisa's historical development toward labor repression, oligarchy, racism and poverty. It may be important, as some have argued, to know the "social origins" of planters, in order to understand their goals, values, beliefs, or world view. It is even more important perhaps to recognize the extension of this world view into the legislatures and courts in the form of laws which supported the planters' dominant value system. However, Louisa's social order did not rest merely upon what planters wanted; labor found ways to limit planter power. Above all, the man-land relationship stood at the center of the social order. That is to say, class rule did not persist in Louisa decade after decade, well into the twentieth century because the ruling class composed former slaveowners who managed to get the law on their side.

Patronage is the term I have used to describe the full range of economic, political, and social relationships in Louisa. It was the foundation, the invisable hand, the *modus operandi* of Louisa's social order. The division of relationships into these three categories, of course, is merely to facilitate study and understanding; Louisa's real social order was integrated. Indeed, expressions of patronage in each sphere of life brought efficacy and legitimacy to the entire patronage system. Economically, patronage assumed the role of a surplus extraction structure, replacing slavery and the paternalistic order with a more formal, contractual, and legalistic system for squeezing labor, and enhancing the profits of capital. Politically, patronage functioned on a different level—patron to patron—as former slaveholders took control of government and served one another at the Feast of the Emancipation, not a sumptuous affair but a far cry from a sharecropper's supper. Socially, patronage might mean the tip of a

99

laborer's hat as a sign of homage to his patron or excessive adulation paid by a planter to his field hand for completion of a task, a kind of social gamemanship practiced by both patron and client to improve productivity or conditions of work. The efficacy of the patronage system was also increased as a result of the patrons' shortages of credit and cash and the clients' lack of alternative employment opportunities, common problems to the postwar South, as well as Louisa. Patronage served the interests of everyone from top to bottom and provided little incentive, therefore, to change or challenge the existing social order.

Poverty became a central feature of Louisa's economy, basically a surplus-extraction structure. The Civil War did not break up previous inequalities of wealth nor destroy the system of class rule. The same elite continued to command the factors of production and preside over their distribution, even extend their collective influence. No evidence supports the claim that class rule "stifled initiative," at least among black farmers.[2] Indeed, the very opposite was the case—hardship produced an even greater determination to succeed, as evidenced by the sacrifices of many black families to become landowners. However, class dominance was stifling in other ways. The mobility of the unlanded (beyond petty holdings of 24 acres, on the average, of thin soil) was severely limited by the monopoly of major income-generating factors, access to which was often through the economic elite. Through the system of clientage, the elite channeled economic growth into areas which benefited the wealthy at the expense of overall prosperity. Investments in bonds to avoid taxes, liquidation of small parts of large estates, the shift to grass farming, and the marketing of their produce outside the county were self-serving responses to status threats not at all beneficial to the population at large.

In a sense, one of the most significant causes of rural poverty was rural poverty itself. Workers accommodated themselves to the demands of employers as part of a general strategy of survival, and each accommodation left them more deeply encumbered and less able or willing to accept the risk of challenging or severing these relationships. Greater independence, such as alternative sources of credit or more equitable distribution of land, machinery, livestock, and oxen (less poverty) would have reduced the risks of resistance by lowering or disbursing the costs. Instead, the life chances of individual laborers lay almost entirely in the hands of a limited range of local patrons. Some did resist through migration or acts of violence, but these individual responses did little to improve laborers' collective economic position. Most stayed and forced whatever concessions they could out of employers without jeopardizing their future security.

Poverty also had political roots, if only because those who dominated Louisa's economic system controlled its political life as well. Economic change was a genuine threat to those at the top, and their political response was to replicate the economic patronage system in still another realm. The county treasury siphoned funds from Louisa residents and then funneled a large portion of tax revenue into the hands of the wealthy in the form of salaries and fees. Ironically, the more extensive poverty became, the more it benefited local patrons, such as physicians, merchants, landowners, and lawyers who were called on to serve as overseers of the poor, transport the indigent to the almshouse, or sell supplies to be furnished to poor families. In addition, the elite were paid for numerous other services not related to poverty but paid out of county funds. Tax breaks for the wealthy and higher rates of taxation for the poor were also part of the political system, as was the rotation in county offices of the same elite, most of whom had been former slaveowners.

Patronage politics perpetuated the maldistribution of wealth which had originated under slavery and kept productive factors from being more widely distributed and the mobility of workers correspondingly limited. Politics in the South as a quest for political office may have been overstudied while the dynamics of local political life have been grossly neglected. Elections for president, governor, senator, representative, or even state legislator seldom touched directly the lives of local residents because of the undemocratic nature of the local political system, and to view politics merely as an expression of representative government hardly seems worthy of so much attention. More important may have been the role of local leaders in giving definition to an entire social structure. In Louisa, the leadership placed the political system at the disposal of the wealthy and directly across the path of democratic social and economic change. This was the political foundation of poverty.

Rural poverty also had racial roots. This may seem a surprising argument in Louisa, where freedmen made remarkable gains after the war, perhaps greater than in most southern counties. Yet, circumstantial evidence supports this hypothesis: white renters in Louisa farmed more land, used more fertilizer, and employed more outside labor, all of which suggests racial discrimination in tenure and credit arrangements.[3] Black achievements were made possible through family sacrifice, and those who succeeded did so not because racism did not exist, but in spite of it. In fact, black renters made greater gains than white renters, who had significant advantages in productive factors.

Racial differences emerge in a number of other areas. Black farmers constituted 52 percent of the population but owned 11 percent of the land in 1900. The land they owned, 24 acres on the average, was poorer than white land, according to state audit reports. Even greater differences appear in black control over productive factors of livestock, draft animals, and personal property. The last agricultural census before the twentieth century showed that one-third of the black farmer sample population owned no draft stock at all, compared with 8 percent of the white farmer sample. Those black farmers who had draft animals depended primarily upon the ox. Mules and horses were more expensive to own and care for. Finally, and most importantly for Louisa, landownership brought neither independence from local patrons nor prosperity to its holders. Instead, Louisa witnessed a dramatic growth of landpoor petty holders with scarcely a hoe to scratch their thin soil.

Moreover, racism and poverty were related in complex ways. Racism was not independent of the economic system, not simply an ideology which sustained itself solely on the myths and dogmas of the past. Rather, its roots were embedded in the economic system of class dominance, which subordinated both a class and a race simultaneously. The blacks' inability to gain greater independence from the white monopolists of wealth and power created an environment tailor-made for the ascription and elaboration of racial stereotypes. The economic dependency of the black population allowed employers to continue to treat their laborers as slaves, call them "their darkies," refer to their wages as "rations," issue them distinctive clothing (oznaburg), "settle up" at Christmas time, place them in crude cabins, and label their resistance as laziness and proof of the need for continued white dominance. Thus, the economic system and race subordination interacted in powerful and mutually supportive ways. When white hegemony was threatened, racism could be appealed to directly or legalized, as it was all over the South after 1890, to thwart the mobility of a significant part of the population.[4] More work is needed to "prove" this hypothesis, but a study of the dynamics of race and class promises to enlarge our understanding of both the origin and trajectory of racism and its impact upon southern life and character.

Besides economic, political, and racial foundations, poverty in

Louisa also had demographic roots. The demographic history of the South has yet to be written, but the evidence from Louisa indicates much can be learned from vital statistics, especially when rates of birth, marriage, and death, household composition, and population growth are set in a local context. The demographic profile of the sample population reveals a highly fertile population with large numbers of children to be supported by each productive worker. Large families and a growing population required a productive agriculture. Demographic forces, of course, do not account for failures to increase production, but they were important on the aggregate demand side of the equation, as increasing numbers of youth came of age to find work and support for their families. The demographic dimension of rural poverty was especially acute within the black farm population, with more women of childbearing age who married at slightly younger ages and therefore produced more children than white women. Blacks responded to these pressures to produce more through adjustments in household composition and greater utilization of the family as a labor unit. Both racial groups responded in a classic way by migrating to other areas. Thus, demographic realities, especially when coupled with the conditions discussed above, contributed in important ways to poverty and are deserving of much more attention by historians of the South.

In 1865 Louisa County stood on the brink of truly revolutionary change. The Civil War had given the old order a series of severe shocks. The courthouse witnessed a manifold reduction in personal property revenues due to the loss of chattel property in the form of freed slaves and destroyed livestock. Patrimonial estates with large investments in slaves, typically half of their total worth, experienced great losses in testate property and the end of its natural accumulation. The labor supply necessary for a labor-intensive, nonmechanized agriculture of corn, tobacco, wheat, and oats could no longer be taken for granted or compelled to work. War and federal reconstruction created a period of political uncertainty. In spite of these jolts, the story of Louisa is one of a missing revolution. The political and economic leadership successfully averted the drastic changes which these developments seemed to portend and staked their hopes for stability upon caste and class. The awful legacy of their resistance to change was poverty and racism, which not only was to threaten the integrity of their own households but those of generations of Louisans to come, and the curse of fathers and mothers was visited upon sons and daughters.

Appendix: Methodology

.

I have used samples extensively in this study to handle large bodies of material over an extended period. Louisa County had over three thousand families after the Civil War. Even with the aid of modern technology, like the computer, I could not study every household, read every will or deed, or handle the seventy volumes of personal property and land tax records between 1865 and 1900. Moreover, there was no need to scrutinize every document. One does not have to read every will to understand how property was divided or to figure out the customary practices of estate probation. A sample of wills at various intervals will reveal just as much. So long as one is sensitive to the biases of samples and makes those biases clear to others, sampling is a legitimate technique to employ when dealing with otherwise unmanageable bodies of data.

Initially, my interest centered on the social history of black farmers in Louisa County during the Reconstruction period, which I wanted to study not merely in general statistical terms but as households and families over time. The federal manuscript censuses of population were the only records available that provided information on black families by household. Since the 1880 census was recognized as the most reliable census after the war (1900 had not been opened to the public when the study began), I decided to use this census as a starting point. A data sheet was designed to match the census categories of information. The data sheet also included columns whereby family numbers could be assigned to each household and each member of the household. Other categories of information which could be derived from the census were added later. Upon this data sheet was recorded all the information the 1880 census of population provided on blacks whose occupation was listed as "farmer"—a total of 663 black families in 1880. This proved to be far more than I anticipated and an unmanageable number, I felt, to try and trace through other censuses. Moreover, I also concluded that white "farmers" ought to be included as a basis of comparison.

Using the same data sheet, I went back through the 1880 census of population and recorded information on every tenth black and white household whose head had an occupation listed as "farmer." The sample produced 265 white and 290 black households and is referred to throughout this study as the "farmer" sample. I also devised a codebook whereby nonnumeric data, such as race or sex, might be recorded numerically.

Using this list of 265 white and 290 black names, I began to add data on each household from various sources. Another date sheet was devised to gather information on these "farmers" from the 1880 agricultural schedules, and additional codes were added to my codebook. This process was repeated for the 1870 census of population and agriculture and the 1900 census of population, when it became available. Information on the 265 white and 290 black householders from land and personal property tax records was added to the census data. In the case of tax records, the years 1870, 1880, 1890, and 1899 were arbitrarily chosen as the sample years.

Eventually, all these sources yielded nearly five computer cards of information on each household (see below). After I had keypunched the information on cards, I began to analyze this mass of data, using Norman H. Nie, *et al., The Statistical Package for the Social Sciences* (New York: McGraw, 1975).

I also had to determine what the 1880 enumerators meant when they listed "farmer" as an occupation. As Merle Curti noted in *The Making of an American Community* (Stanford: Stanford Univ. Press, 1959), those listed as owners on the agricultural schedule included all persons in charge of a working farm, even if they were renters or absentee managers. In addition, many of those whose occupation was listed as "farmer" on the population schedule I could not locate on the schedule of agriculture. Finally, a "farm" in the census definition excluded all those holdings under three acres (see Curti, pp. 59–60, 455–56). Tax records used in conjunction with the census schedules, however, permitted positive identification of actual owners, as long as two or more persons of identical names did not appear on the landbooks. When this happened in the case of my sample, I had to eliminate that person from any analysis which might be affected by the uncertainty of tenure. Thus, in order to qualify as an owner in this study, an individual case had to meet both of the following conditions: occupation must be given as "farmer" on the population schedule, and the person's name had to appear on the

land taxbook of Louisa County. Furthermore, since it is obvious
that the census meant to distinguish the "farmer without a farm"
from both the owner and the laborer, in cases where the agricultural schedule called the individual an operator and where that same
individual could not be located on the land records of the county,
I have assumed that he was a tenant.

A comparison of the number listed by the agricultural schedule
as owners with those actually found on the landbooks suggests the
extent to which census records have exaggerated the number of
farm owners. On the 1880 agricultural census schedule, 58 percent of the sample of white farmers ($N = 165$) and 34 percent
of the sample of black farmers ($N = 86$) might be construed as
owners. In fact, in that year I found only 40 percent of the white
sample and 11 percent of the black sample on the local landbooks.

Since my initial base sample is not a random sample of the
entire population, but a random sample of those whose occupation was listed as "farmer," I suspect that poverty in Louisa
County was even worse than this study at times indicates. As I
pointed out in the chapter on clients, day laborers were the most
vulnerable members of the labor force, and my sample may have
underrepresented them. However, day laborers tended to leave
the county if they were unsuccessful in acquiring property, and
thus my initial sample may have become more representative over
time.

In the case of the 1900 manuscript census of population, I also
selected a totally random sample of Louisans and collected data on
them, in addition to the 1880 sample "farmers." For this sample, I
chose every tenth person and recorded all the information the
census provided. This sample yielded a total of 304 householders,
and it proved useful for making generalizations about Louisa at
the turn of the century.

I also used sampling techniques for will and deedbooks, reading
approximately 125 wills and deeds. Although I read many wills
and deeds of members of the "farmer" sample, I made no deliber-
ate effort to confine myself to the sample. Rather, I chose wills
and deeds randomly at ten-year intervals. Wills provided information on the customary practices of estate probation and occasionally included complete inventories of estates. Deeds illuminated
the operation of the lien system. All lien agreements were
required by law to be recorded at the courthouse, although many
appear not to have been so recorded. I used the index of deeds to

gauge the frequency of lien agreements over the period and to assess the general trends in official lien agreements.

Except in wills and deeds, racial identities were usually given. The federal census records, of course, always identified the race of members of households. Personal property and land taxbooks also included the race of property holders. Even when race was not included, as in the case of wills or deeds, or the Board of Supervisors' journal, or the plantation records of Thomas S. Watson, or the few extant copies of the local newspaper, it could usually be derived. Political leaders whose names I did not recognize could usually be found in tax records that gave race. Often, they could also be located in willbooks before the war and identified as slaveholders. A list of doctors and dentists found in the courthouse identified still other white leaders. Also, working with hundreds of names in all of these records, I gradually became familiar with or could eventually find the racial identities of most Louisans. A small but important clue to racial identity proved to be the absence of middle initials of names. Nearly all of the cases of missing middle initials turned out to be black Louisans.

I used property holding as the basis of class identity in Louisa. Land and personal property taxbooks were invaluable sources for discussing the distribution of wealth. They provided the data for identifying the top 5 percent of property holders. Changes in the distribution of wealth at different periods were gauged by examining the records at ten-year intervals and identifying the top 5 percent at each interval. The answer to the question of the distribution of wealth in Louisa proved central to understanding the period.

In chapter six, I used the data I had gathered from land and personal property tax records on householders to form an "index of economic status" for each household. In constructing the index, I included five variables: land, machinery, draft animals, livestock, and furniture. For each variable, the "farmer" sample population was divided into fourths, based on the assessed value of each individual's property. Since my base year was 1870, the index is in terms of assessed values for 1870. A number between 0 and 3 was assigned to each fourth, the number increasing as a household's value of a particular resource increased.

The index of economic status is a sum of the rank-figures for each variable. For example, if a family had a rank of 3 for land, 2 for machinery, 4 for livestock, 2 for draft animals, and 3 for furniture, its index number would be 14. After an index was computed for each white family, the families were grouped into four quartiles (or as close as possible): lower quartile, second quartile, third quartile, and an upper quartile. This ranking of white families became a standard for ranking black families.

			Values (in dollars) of Draft		
Rank	Land	Machinery	Animals	Livestock	Furniture
0	0	0	0	0	0
1	1–472	1–10	1–75	1–75	1–50
2	473–2,150	11–50	76–200	76–200	51–100
3	Over 2,150	51–500	201–1,000	201–1,300	101–1,000

Also, in chapter six, the number of cases in some cells of the tables were so small as to call into question whether chance might not produce the same results. This difficulty often arises in samples of small size where the differences between two subpopulations, in my case between blacks and whites, may at times be quite narrow. In order to determine the probability that chance had produced the indicated results in the cells of my tables, I used tests of statistical significance. Fortunately, others have experienced similar difficulties and I found a convenient table for samples of various sizes. It is based upon the laws of probability and provides a handy test of when percentage differences between population subgroups of various sizes reflect genuine population differences, and when the percentage differences might have been produced by chance. For the table and an explanation of sampling error and statistical significance, see Gerhard Lenski, "Appendix I: Sampling Error and Statistical Significance," in Lenski, *The Religious Factor* (New York: Doubleday, 1963), 367–76.

In 1880, the federal censuses enumerated deaths by county, giving name, age, sex, race, and cause of death for each person. Since this appeared to be a more complete record of death than the county registration of deaths (1864–71), it was used in chapter six in my discussion of mortality. In the course of that discussion, I refer to racial differences in death rates by age. These generalizations required a series of steps. First, I used the 1880 census figures to form a table of the age-race-sex distribution of deaths. Upon reducing this table to a percentage distribution, I could then calculate indices of dissimilarity and relative composition from which my summary statements are derived.

An index of dissimilarity is designed to show how different one population is from another without specifying just how they differ.

By using a percent distribution as a standard of comparison (in this case, the total column) and subtracting from it all of the other columns, recording only the differences, I produced a set of percentage point differences. The index of dissimilarity is the sum of percentage point differences of like sign.

Still, this index is not the step from which generalizations may be made safely because the index of dissimilarity does not make allowance for the size of the base percentages. In other words, the percentage point differences may be small because the base percentage is small. Yet, these small differences might be quite significant. One needs an index that takes this into consideration. By dividing each percentage point difference by the base point (i.e., in my case the total column) and multiplying by 100, a new index—the index of relative composition—may be formed which solves the problem of small percentages.

The index of relative composition forms the basis of my statements, for example, about the percentages of blacks who succumbed to infant mortality compared with the total population (the standard of comparison). This index corrects for the problem of small percentage point differences. Demographers recognize the index of relative composition as the best index for comparing two populations. For a more detailed discussion of these techniques, see Donald J. Bogue, *Principles of Demography* (New York: Wiley, 1969), 115–18. Table A.2 shows the steps involved leading up to the index of relative composition.

Unfortunately, my study does not have as strong a temporal perspective as I would have liked. In part, this is due to my data collection at ten-year intervals, where change is difficult to date precisely. More importantly, temporal changes in a study of this kind are not dramatic events, like a slave revolt or a political revolution. In Louisa, revolutionary changes occurred, but they were quiet revolutions which took place over extended periods. Black labor left the county, former slaveholders shifted to grass farming, freedmen acquired land, patronage weakened—all significant changes, but they took place gradually and sometimes simultaneously. Their significance is not diminished in the least by the pace of change.

Critics of local studies might argue that county studies provide only a limited view of history, that no county "represents" the South. As I noted in the Preface, no county is statistically representative of the southern region. However, this kind of statistical representativeness is not important. More significantly, Louisa does represent processes of social change common to the postwar South. Furthermore, until more local studies are done, the extent to which Louisa represents the South, or for that matter, the South represents Louisa cannot be determined. The difficulties and limitations of local history cannot be used as an argument to justify ignoring the local area without imperiling our deeper understanding of the past. When southern counties finally become the subject of more American social historians, I believe the historians will find much more evidence of poverty and patronage.

Table A.1   Data for Each Case, Louisa County "Farmer" Sample, 1870–1900 by Computer Card and Column Number (five cards per "case" or household)

CARD 1

IBM Column Number	Data	IBM Column Number	Data
1	Life cycle	41	Race
2	Tenure	42	Sex of head of HH
3–5	Improved acreage—1880	43–44	Age—1880
6–8	Total acreage—1880	45	Marital status—1880
9–10	Land value—1880	46–47	Occupation—1880
11	Machinery value—1880	48	Attended school—1880
12–13	Livestock value—1880	49	Literacy—1880
14	Fertilizer—1880	50–51	Birthplace
15–16	Labor cost—1880	52–53	Type strangers in HH—1880
17–18	Amount produced—1880	54	No. horses—1880
19	Decade of mother's birth	55	No. mules—1880
20–21	Household size—1880	56	No. Oxen—1880
22	District—1880	57	Primary livestock—1880
23	Males 17 & over—1880	58	Secondary livestock—1880
24	Males und. 17—1880	59	Tertiary livestock—1880
25	Females 17 & over—1880	60–61	Primary crop—1880
26	Females under 17—1880	62–64	Yield/acre, primary crop—1880
27–28	Family size—1880	65–66	Secondary crop—1880
29–30	Type family—1880	67–69	Yield/acre, secondary crop—1880
31–32	No. empl. in HH—1880	70–71	Tertiary crop—1880
33–36	Family number	72–74	Yield/acre, tertiary crop—1880
37–38	Identification no.	75–77	Dozens eggs produced—1880
39–40	Relationship to head of HH—1880	78–80	Pounds butter produced—1880

CARD 2

IBM Column Number	Data		Data
1–4	Acres landbook—1879	11–14	Acres landbook—1890
5–6	Value/acre inc. bldgs.—1879	15–16	Value/acre incl. bldgs.—1890
7–10	Value of bldgs.—1879	17–20	Value of bldgs.—1890

Note: HH means household.

CARD 2

IBM Column

Number	Data		
21–24	Acres landbook—1899	55	No. oxen—1870
25–26	Value/acre incl. bldgs.—1899	56	Primary livestock—1870
27–30	Value of bldgs.—1899	57	Secondary livestock—1870
31–32	(blank)	58	Tertiary livestock—1870
33–36	Family number	59–60	Livestock value—1870
37–39	Consumer/worker ratio—1880	61–62	Primary crop—1870
40–42	Improved acres—1870	63–64	Secondary crop—1870
43–45	Unimproved acres—1870	65–66	Tertiary crop—1870
46–47	Bushels of peas and beans—1870	67–68	Tons of hay—1870
48–49	Farm value—1870	69–71	Pounds butter—1870
50	Machinery value—1870	72–73	Value animals sold—1870
51–52	Wages and board paid—1870	74–75	Total value farm produce—1870
53	No. horses—1870		
54	No. mules—1870	76–80	(blank)

CARD 3

IBM Column

Number	Data		
1–4	Family number	44–45	Total tax—1890
5	HH Size—1870	46–47	Value draft animals—1899
6	Family size—1870	48–49	Primary livestock—1899
7–8	Family type—1870	50–51	Secondary livestock—1899
9–10	Occupation—1870	52–53	Tertiary livestock—1899
11	Developmental cycle—1870	54–55	Livestock value—1899
12–13	People in HH 1870 but not 1880	56	Machinery value—1899
14–15	People in HH 1880 but not 1870	57–58	Furniture value—1899
16–17	Strangers in HH 1870	59–60	Total tax—1899
18–22	Real estate value—1870	61–62	Value draft animals—1870
23–27	Personal property value 1870	63–64	Primary livestock—1870
28–30	Consumer/worker ratio—1870	65–66	Secondary livestock—1870
31–32	Value draft animals—1890	67–68	Tertiary livestock—1870
33–34	Primary livestock—1890	69–70	Livestock value—1870
35–36	Secondary livestock—1890	71	Machinery value—1870
37–38	Tertiary livestock—1890	72–73	Furniture value—1870
39–40	Livestock value—1890	74–75	Total tax—1870
41	Machinery value—1890	76–80	(blank)
42–43	Furniture value—1890		

CARD 4

IBM Column

Number	Data		
1–4	Family number	11–13	Consumer/worker ratio—1900
5–6	HH size—1900	14	Developmental cycle—1900
7–8	Family size—1900	15–16	Strangers in HH—1900
9–10	Type HH—1900	17–18	Occupation of head—1900

CARD 4
IBM Column
Number Data

19–20	Wife occupation—1900	35–36	No. children ever—1900
21–22	Occupation of son—1900	37	Home ownership—1900
23–24	Occupation of son—1900	38–39	Husband's age at marriage
25–26	Occupation of son—1900	40–41	Wife's age at marriage
27–28	Occupation of dau.—1900	42–43	Year of marriage
29–30	Occupation of dau.—1900	44–45	Occupation—1900
31–32	Occupation of dau.—1900	46	No. marriage
33–34	No. employed in HH—1900	47	Marriage cohort
		48–80	(blank)

CARD 5
IBM Column
Number   Data

1–4	Family number	26	Persistence
5–6	Value draft animals—1880	27	Index of market integration—1870
7	Primary livestock—1880	28	Index of market integration—1880
8	Secondary livestock—1880	29	Cf. 1870 to 1880 index of market
9	Tertiary livestock—1880		integration
10–11	Livestock value—1880	30–31	Percent of improved acres in
12	Machinery value—1880		tobacco—1880
13–14	Furniture value—1880	32–33	Percent of improved acres in
15–16	Total tax—1880		corn—1880
17–18	Land tenure chg—1870–1900	34–35	Percent of improved acres in
19	Loss, gain, or same acreage—		wheat—1880
	1870–1900	36–37	Percent of improved acres in
20–21	Personal property gain—		oats—1880
	1870–1900	38–39	Percent of improved acres
22–23	Personal property loss—1870—1900		fallow—1880
24–25	Most valuable resource at 1st residence	40–80	(blank)

Table A.2 Distribution of Census Deaths, by Age, Sex, and Race, Louisa County, 1880

	Total Deaths	White Male	White Female	Black Male	Black Female
Total	350	51	48	120	131
Under 1	83	8	6	38	31
1–10	23	7	3	7	6
11–18	51	6	6	18	21
19–24	32	1	3	11	17
25–34	25	2	3	5	15
35–44	17	2	3	6	6
45–54	33	7	2	6	18
55–64	25	4	7	9	5
65–74	26	8	9	6	3
75 +	35	6	6	14	9

Source: Ms Census, Social Statistics, Louisa County, 1880.

Table A.3 Percentage Distribution of Census Deaths, by Age, Sex, and Race, Louisa County, 1880

	All Deaths	White Male	White Female	Black Male	Black Female
Total	100.0	100.0	100.0	100.0	100.0
Under 1	23.7	15.7	12.5	31.7	23.7
1–10	14.6	11.8	12.5	15.0	16.0
11–18	6.6	13.7	6.3	5.8	4.6
19–24	9.1	2.0	6.3	9.2	13.0
25–34	7.1	3.9	6.3	4.2	11.5
35–44	4.9	3.9	6.3	5.0	4.6
45–54	9.4	13.7	4.2	5.0	13.7
55–64	7.1	7.8	14.6	7.5	3.8
65–74	7.4	15.7	18.8	5.0	2.3
75 +	10.0	11.8	12.5	11.7	6.9

Source: Ms Census, Social Statistics, Louisa County, 1880.

Table A.4   Index of Dissimilarity, Census Deaths, Louisa
County, 1880

Percent Point Differences

	White Male	White Female	Black Male	Black Female
All	0.0	0.0	0.0	0.0
Under 1	− 8.0	− 11.2	+ 8.0	0.0
1–10	− 2.8	− 2.1	+ .4	+ 1.4
11–18	+ 7.1	− .3	− .8	− 2.0
19–24	− 7.1	− 2.8	+ .1	+ 3.9
25–34	− 3.2	− .8	− 2.9	+ 4.4
35–44	− 1.0	+ 1.4	+ .1	− .3
45–54	+ 4.3	− 5.2	− 4.4	+ 4.3
55–64	+ .7	+ 7.5	+ .4	− 3.3
65–74	+ 8.3	+ 11.4	− 2.4	− 5.1
75 +	+ 1.8	+ 2.5	+ 1.7	− 3.1
Index of Dissimilarity				
	22.2	22.8	10.7	14.0

Source: Ms Census, Social Statistics, Louisa County, 1880.

Note: Minuses and pluses not equal due to rounding error. Positive values were used for the index of dissimilarity.

Table A.5   Index of Relative Composition, Census Deaths,
Louisa County, 1880

	White Male	White Female	Black Male	Black Female
Under 1	− 33.8	− 47.3	+ 33.8	0.0
1–10	− 19.2	− 14.3	+ 2.7	+ 9.6
11–18	+ 107.6	− 4.5	− 12.1	− 30.3
19–24	− 78.0	− 30.8	+ 1.1	+ 42.9
25–34	− 45.1	− 11.3	− 40.8	+ 62.0
35–44	− 20.4	+ 28.6	+ 2.0	− 6.1
45–54	+ 45.7	− 55.3	− 46.8	+ 45.7
55–64	+ 9.9	+ 105.6	+ 5.6	− 46.5
65–74	+ 112.2	+ 154.1	− 32.4	− 68.9
75 +	+ 18.0	+ 25.0	+ 17.0	− 31.0

Source: Ms Census, Social Statistics, Louisa County, 1880.

Note: Minuses and pluses not equal due to rounding error.

Table A.6 Population, Improved Acreage, and Value of
Productive Factors, Louisa and Selected Counties,
1860 and 1900

1860

County	Pop.	Imp. Acres	Farms (value in dollars)	Machinery	Livestock
Louisa (Va.)	16,701	156,950	4,461,836	108,245	556,856
Greene (Ga.)	12,651	120,165	1,855,185	108,946	424,107
Hamilton (Ia.)	1,699	8,237	312,375	14,860	53,115
Trempealeau (Wi.)	2,560	11,509	367,240	12,516	78,632

1900

County	Pop.	Imp. Acres	Farms (value in dollars)	Machinery	Livestock
Louisa (Va.)	16,517	111,889	364,197	97,630	387,710
Greene (Ga.)	16,542	91,666	255,714	89,400	265,425
Hamilton (Ia.)	19,514	328,308	2,630,989	595,720	2,704,918
Trempealeau (Wi.)	23,114	253,343	1,746,728	560,110	1,804,619

Source: General Tables, U.S. Census, 1860 and 1900. See Source, Table 1.1, for more specific references.

Table A.7   Major Crops, Livestock, and Produce, Louisa
County, 1860–1900

Item	Unit of measurement	1860	1870	1880	1900
Hay	acres	9,559	886	2,131	4,950
Tobacco	acres	5,998	1,162	2,978	2,647
Maize	acres	19,184	7,597	23,807	24,005
Wheat	acres	25,826	12,635	11,928	6,381
Oats	acres	11,007	8,425	10,329	3,294
Horses	each	2,485	1,734	2,167	3,169
Milch Cows	each	3,050	2,375	3,357	3,725
Other Cows	each	4,377	1,658	3,360	4,428
Sheep	each	7,674	2,088	4,001	3,872
Swine	each	16,259	6,354	11,224	10,851
Eggs	dozen	-	-	106,949	257,520
Butter	pounds	93,860	75,914	118,174	181,790
Milch	gallons (sold)	-	-	851	7,315

Source: General tables, U.S. Census, 1860–1900. See Source, Table 1.1 for more specific references. Crop figures for 1860 and 1870, which were given in pounds, bushels, or tons, were translated into acres in order to make the table comparable. Average yields, as indicated by federal agricultural reports of the period, were used to derive acreages. These were: tobacco—800 pounds/acre; maize—20 bushels/acre; wheat—10 bushels/acre; oats—15 bushels/acre; hay—1.3 tons/acre.

Notes

.

NOTES TO THE PREFACE

1. For example, Philip J. Greven, Jr., *Four Generations: Population, Land, and Family in Colonial Andover, Massachusetts* (Ithaca: Cornell Univ. Press, 1969); Kenneth A. Lockridge, *A New England Town: The First Hundred Years* (New York: Norton, 1970); Frank Cancian, *Change and Uncertainty in a Peasant Economy: The Maya Corn Farmers of Zinacantan* (Stanford: Stanford Univ. Press, 1972); Allen W. Johnson, *Sharecroppers of the Sertão: Economics and Dependence on a Brazilian Plantation* (Stanford: Stanford Univ. Press, 1971); Julian A. Pitt-Rivers, *The People of the Sierra* (Chicago: Univ. of Chicago Press, 1971); Susan Tax Freeman, *Neighbors: The Social Contract in a Castilian Hamlet* (Chicago: Univ. of Chicago Press, 1970); E. J. Hobsbawm and George Rudé, *Captain Swing* (New York: Pantheon, 1968); W. G. Hoskins, *The Midland Peasant* (London: Macmillan, 1957); Edward C. Banfield, *The Moral Basis of a Backward Society* (New York: Free Press, 1958); and Emmaneul Le Roy Ladurie, *The Peasants of Languedoc,* trans. John Day (Urbana: Univ. of Illinois Press, 1974).

2. See Maurice R. Stein, *The Eclipse of Community: An Interpretation of American Studies* (New York: Harper, 1960), esp. 3–5.

3. See Kenneth M. Stampp, *The Peculiar Institution: Slavery in the Ante-Bellum South* (New York: Vintage, 1956), esp. ch. 9; Alfred H. Conrad and John R. Meyers, "The Economics of Slavery in the Ante Bellum South," *Journal of Political Economy* 66 (Apr. 1958): 95–130; Allan Nevins, *Ordeal of the Union,* vol. I (New York, 1947), 438; and Barrington Moore, Jr., *Social Origins of Dictatorship and Democracy: Lord and Peasant in the Making of the Modern World* (Boston: Beacon, 1966), ch. 3. Moore asks, "After all was not the plantation owner just another capitalist?" He also points out that labor-repressive agricultural systems, like plantation slavery, pose obstacles only to particular kinds of capitalism (121, 152).

4. *Roll, Jordon, Roll: The World the Slaves Made* (New York: Pantheon, 1974), 4–7, 661–65.

5. *The Burden of Southern History* (Baton Rouge: Louisiana State Univ. Press, 1977), esp. ch. 9.

6. See Jonathan M. Wiener, "Class Structure and Economic Development in the American South, 1865–1955," including Robert Higgs and Harold D. Woodman's "Comments" and a "Reply" by Wiener, all in "Forum," *American Historical Review* 84, no. 4 (Oct. 1979): 970–1006.

NOTES TO CHAPTER I

1. Malcolm H. Harris, *History of Louisa County, Virginia* (Richmond, Va.: Dietz, 1936), 1–13.

2. Paul W. Gates, *The Farmer's Age: Agriculture, 1815–1860*, vol. III: *The Economic History of the United States,* Henry David *et al.,* eds. (New York: Harper and Row, 1960), 100–7.

3. *Ibid.,* 104.

4. *Ibid.,* 102.

5. *Ibid.,* 104–6.

6. U. S. Bureau of the Census, *Ninth Census, 1870: Population,* table 2, pp. 68–70.

7. Gates, *The Farmer's Age,* 107–8.

8. Avery Craven, *Soil Exhaustion as a Factor in the Agricultural History of Virginia and Maryland, 1606–1860* (Urbana: Univ. of Illinois Press, 1926). Craven is challenged by Gates, *The Farmer's Age,* 109–10.

9. *Ninth Census: Population, 1870,* table 2, pp. 68–70.

10. Gates, *The Farmer's Age,* 110.

11. In 1860 there were 765 slaveholders and 1,217 white families in Louisa and 10,194 slaves in a total population of 16,701. When free blacks are added to the slave population, Louisa County was 63 percent black in 1860. U. S. Bureau of the Census, *Eighth Census, 1860: Agriculture,* 244; and *ibid., Statistics,* 350; Stampp, *Peculiar Institution,* 30.

12. Personal Property Taxbook, Louisa County, 1863, Virginia State Library, Richmond, Va. (hereafter, PP. Book and the year). Total revenue for 1863 was $102,699, and slaves were evaluated at $5.8 million of the total $8.2 million worth of personal property.

13. Louisa Willbook, 15: 21–25, 178–85. These cases were chosen from the wills recorded in the county in 1859 as examples of the importance of slave wealth to large landowners, but they show a good deal more. Eugene D. Genovese once characterized the slave economy as precapitalistic and unlike the rational capitalism of the

industrialized North. Investments, not only in human flesh but in bonds and other securities, reflected in these wills seriously call into question that conclusion and support the judgment of Barrington Moore, Jr., that indeed, southern planters were hard-nosed, calculating businessmen, not unlike northern industrialists. See Eugene D. Genovese, *The Political Economy of Slavery* (New York: Random, 1965), and Moore, *Social Origins*, 111– 55. It has also been argued that slave "breeding" was a practice of border states' planters, who engaged in this practice to take advantage of the higher prices which slaves commanded in the lower South between 1850 and 1860. See Richard Sutch, "The Breeding of Slaves for Sale and the Westward Expansion of Slavery, 1850–1860," 173–210; for critical comments on Sutch's argument, see "A Critique of Sutch on 'The Breeding of Slaves,'" 527–30, and Eugene D. Genovese, "Concluding Remarks," 531–39, all in Stanley L. Engerman and Eugene D. Genovese, eds. *Race and Slavery in the Western Hemisphere: Quantitative Studies* (Princeton: Princeton Univ. Press, 1975).

14. Holders of 1–10 slaves composed 55 percent of Louisa's slaveholders. See *Eighth Census, 1860: Agriculture*, 244. Kenneth M. Stampp has argued that nearly three-fourths of all southern slaveholders were smallholders of 1–10 slaves, thereby discrediting the mythology of the South as a land of large slaveholding. See Stampp, *Peculiar Institution*, 20.

15. The choice of these particular counties as a basis of comparison was not arbitrary. Rather, they were selected because they have been the subjects of other studies, which gave me a good deal more information about their history and development than would have been the case with a totally random selection. See Robert Preston Brooks, *The Agrarian Revolution in Georgia* (Westport, Conn.: Negro Univ. Press, 1970); Allan G. Bogue, *From Prairie to Corn Belt*, Chicago: Univ. of Chicago Press, 1963); and Merle Curti, *The Making of an American Community: A Case Study of Democracy in a Frontier County* (Stanford: Stanford Univ. Press, 1969). For the actual figures from which these per capita averages were derived, see Appendix.

16. Bogue, *From Prairie*, 14–15.

17. The growth in horsepower in the Midwest was remarkable. The number of horses in Louisa County, Va., fell between 1860 and 1900, from 2,485 to 2,169; in Greene County, Ga., from 1,789 to 1,503. During the same forty years, the count of horses in Hamilton County, Ia., grew from 386 to 13,284, while the count in Trempeauleau County, Wi., underwent a similar explosion, 392 to 10,664. *Eighth Census, 1860: Agriculture*, 22–23, 158, 166–67; *Twelfth Census, 1900: Agriculture*, vol. V, pt. I, pp. 426–27, 487–90.

18. Some of these differences I learned on my grandfather's knee and the rest from Bogue, *From Prairie,* 119–20, and Gates, *The Farmer's Age,* 227–28. The term "well heeled" has a different meaning today. As used here, it refers to a draft animal, like a horse or mule, which is controlled by a bit in the mouth and trained to keep its weight balanced or in the heels so the "front end" pivots easily at the tug of a rein attached to the bit.

19. Gates, *The Farmer's Age,* 227–28; Fred A. Shannon, *The Farmer's Last Frontier: Agriculture 1860–1897,* vol. V: *The Economic History of the United States,* Henry David, *et al.,* eds. (New York: Farrar and Rinehart, 1945), 128.

20. Bogue, *From Prairie,* 119–20, 228.

21. U. S. Bureau of the Census, *Tenth Census of the United States, 1880: Agriculture,* 152, 174, 176.

22. The sample produced 265 black and 290 white households, or about 15.4 percent of all families in Louisa in 1880. It is identified throughout the book as the "farmer" sample to distinguish it from other samples. Information on all these households was accumulated from the 1870 and 1880 federal censuses of population and agriculture, the 1900 federal census of population, and personal property and land taxbooks at decade intervals between 1870 and 1900. Computer analysis of the data was aided by Norman H. Nie, *et al., Statistical Package for the Social Sciences* (New York: McGraw, 1975). See Appendix for further information on the sample.

23. Shannon, *The Farmer's Last Frontier,* 128.

24. See n. 17, above.

25. Bogue, *From Prairie,* 287.

26. *Ibid.,* 286; Louisa Landbook, 1900.

27. Curti, *The Making,* 144. See Appendix for the ranking of Louisa owners.

28. Curti, *The Making,* 145.

29. "What Louisa Did in the War Between the States," address of J. William Jones at Dedication of Confederate Monument at Louisa Courthouse, 17 Aug. 1905, Alderman Library, Univ. of Virginia, Charlottesville, Va.

30. Harris, *History of Louisa,* 96–103.

31. *Ibid.,* 97, 103.

32. PP. Book, 1863 and 1866. These losses support other estimates of war damage in which the devastation and pillaging by invading armies is said to have resulted in the loss of every third horse or mule and nearly one half the agricultural machinery. See C. Vann Woodward, *Origins of the New South, 1877–1913* (Baton Rouge: Louisiana State Univ. Press, 1971), 177. In the cotton South, conditions of war claimed one-third of the horses, asses, and mules;

see Roger L. Ransom and Richard Sutch, *One Kind of Freedom: The Economic Consequences of Emancipation* (Cambridge: Cambridge Univ. Press, 1977), 48. And one-third of the stock of hogs was also lost; see Gavin Wright, *The Political Economy of the Cotton South* (New York: Norton, 1978), 164.

33. PP. Book, 1863. Personal property tax revenue totaled $88,602. A more careful treatment of the exact distribution of county revenues is presented in ch. 5.

34. Landbook and PP. Book, 1863, 1870.

35. For the elaboration of the New South myth into a creed, see Paul M. Gaston, *The New South Creed: A Study in Southern Mythmaking* (New York: Knopf, 1970).

36. Banks, *The Economics of Land Tenure in Georgia* (New York: Columbia Univ. Press, 1905).

37. *Origins of Class Struggle in Louisiana: A Social History of White Farmers and Laborers during Slavery and After, 1840–1875* (Baton Rouge: Louisana State Univ. Press, 1972).

38. Woodward, *Origins,* 179.

39. Wiener, *Social Origins of the New South: Alabama 1860–1885* (Baton Rouge: Louisiana State Univ. Press, 1978), 8–16; and "Planter-Merchant Conflict in Reconstruction Alabama," *Past and Present* 68 (Aug. 1975): 73–94. For additional references, see Wiener, *Social Origins,* 9n, and James L. Roark, *Masters Without Slaves: Southern Planters in the Civil War and Reconstruction* (New York: Norton, 1977), 241n.

40. The table is derived from the landbooks of 1860 and 1870. I simply placed all owners into one of these three categories according to the size of holding as given by the landbooks.

41. See Shugg, *Origins,* 248–69; Woodward, *Origins,* 179–80, where both conclude that prewar planters were replaced after the war; see also Shannon, *The Farmer's Last Frontier,* 80–85. This view is challenged in Wiener, *Social Origins,* 8–9 and n. 8.

42. Louisa Landbook, 1860 and 1870. Precise determination of the actual number of owners was not possible because of the various ways owners were listed on the landbooks. With little else to go on besides names, I found it was not always possible to ascertain, for example, whether M. A. Smith, M. Arthur Smith, or Matthew A. Smith were the same or different owners. The actual number falls somewhere within this range, however. Moreover, the actual persistance rate may have been even greater. Surely death claimed some indeterminate number of largeholders, either by natural causes or on Civil War battlefields, and estates might be transferred to sons and daughters before death. It was impossible to follow these changes, even for a small sample. In these cases, county landbooks

would have recorded the estate in another family member's name in 1870, when the estate had not really left family hands.

43. Cf. Weiner, *Social Origins,* 238, where he found a postwar persistence rate of 63 percent for the economic elite.

44. In 1900, 41 out of the 118 nonresident owners were from New York, other states, unknown residences, and Baltimore, in order of importance. See Louisa Landbook, 1870 and 1900, which recorded the residential address for each landowner. The claim has been made that absentee ownership was "aggravated, intensified, and multiplied" in the South after slavery; Woodward, *Origins,* 180. See also Shugg, *Origins,* 248–49. This was not the case in Louisa. The same claim was made for "soil-mining" and one-crop agriculture, neither of which characterized postwar Louisa. Perhaps these generalizations do not apply to tobacco-growing regions, where the decline in that type of cash-crop farming predated the decline of the cotton culture.

45. In actual numbers, the population appears to have been nearly stable between 1870 and 1900, i.e., 16,332 residents in 1870 and 16,517 in 1900. *Twelfth Census, 1900: Population,* vol. I, pt. I, p. 43. However, the 1880 census enumerated 18,942 residents, so the population did grow over the period. See ch. 3, p. 132n.

46. Louisa Landbook, 1870 and 1900, which noted the race of landowners.

47. In actual acres, blacks owned 36,185 out of a total of 316,023 acres; *Annual Report of the Auditor, September 30, 1900* (Richmond, Va.), table 28. For the racial composition of the population, see *Twelfth Census, 1900: Population,* vol. I, pt. I, pp. 561–62. For total acreage, see Louisa Landbook, 1900.

48. For the number of owners and the percentage of the total acreage the top 5 percent of these owned, see Louisa Landbook, 1860 and 1900; for the number of taxed heads of household and the percentage of total personal property the top 5 percent held, see PP. Book, 1863 and 1900. Although Louisa did not assess a head tax on females, if they held property, they were included on the personal property books, and if they fell into the top 5 percent, they were included here also. What could not be included in the numerator were nonpropertyholding female heads of households. If they could be identified, the concentration would be higher than this estimate. Still, Louisa County's land was not nearly as concentrated as some areas of the cotton South. In Dallas County, Ala., for example, in 1860 the top 5 percent controlled 47.2 percent of all real estate; see Ransom and Sutch, *One Kind,* 79. In Alabama, the top 10 percent of black-belt planters owned 55 percent of the land in 1860 and 63 percent in 1870; see Wiener, *Social Origins,* 15.

49. This generalization is reflected in Table 1.3 in the difference between actual holdings and the 5 percent of all land the top 5 percent would have held under conditions of total equality, a figure of 17 percent in 1860 and 25 percent in 1900. The same trend was found in Alabama. See Wiener, *Social Origins,* 16.

50. These means are based upon the county landbook of 1880, in which acreages were found for each member of the "farmer" sample.

51. I am reminded here especially of Jewish zealots who boldly ventured to plant agricultural communes on cheap lands of the United States, but who failed to take into account their needs for farming implements and machinery, livestock, seed, even homes, as described in Irving Howe, *World of Our Fathers* (New York: Simon and Schuster, 1976), 84–87. I am reminded, too, of all the debate that has centered on the hypothesis, first advanced by Frederick Jackson Turner in 1893, that western lands had served as a "safety valve" for discontented urban laborers of the East. Later estimates were that $1,000 was needed to settle on the frontier, an amount few laborers and only select numbers of immigrants were able to raise; see Marcus Lee Hansen, *The Immigrant in American History* (New York: Harper Torchbooks, 1964), 73–74; see also Bogue, *From Prairie,* esp. 148–49 and 166–68, where it is obvious that to be successful settlers needed much more capital than the purchase price of the land.

52. "Revisionist" historians of the period known as the Reconstruction Era, generally the period 1865–1877, have called the failure to redistribute land the single most glaring oversight of the period. See Vernon Lane Wharton, *The Negro in Mississippi, 1865–1890* (Chapel Hill: Univ. of North Carolina Press, 1947), 38–41; Kenneth M. Stampp, *The Era of Reconstruction, 1865–1877* (New York: Vintage, 1965), 126–31. See also Ransom and Sutch, *One Kind,* 80; Shannon, *The Farmer's Last Frontier,* 79–80; Edward Magdol, *A Right to the Land: Essays on the Freedmen's Community* (Westport, Conn.: Greenwood, 1977), esp. chs. 6–9; Steven Joseph Ross, "Freed Soil, Freed Labor, Freed Men: John Eaton and the Davis Bend Experiment," *Journal of Southern History* 44, no. 2 (May 1978): 213–32; Lawanda Cox, "The Promise of Land for the Freedman," *Mississippi Valley Historical Review* 45 (Dec. 1958): 413–40; William S. McFeely, *Yankee Stepfather: General O. O. Howard and t' e Freedmen* (New Haven: Yale Univ. Press, 1968), esp. chs. 4–8; James M. McPherson, *The Struggle for Equality: Abolitionists and the Negro in the Civil War and Reconstruction* (Princeton: Princeton Univ. Press, 1964), 246–59, 407–16. For further references, see James M. McPherson, *et al., Blacks in America: Bibliographical Essays* (Garden City, N. Y.: Doubleday, 1972), 121–23.

53. For a stimulating discussion of the importance of various productive factors in agriculture, see Theodore Schultz, *Transforming Traditional Agriculture* (New Haven: Yale Univ. Press, 1964).

54. The crucial importance of yield-producing factors to the economic well-being of individual householders will become clearer in ch. 6, where I have analyzed the gains of families at different economic levels over the family life cycle.

55. These life histories were pieced together from the sources listed in p. 120n.

56. Since the date for personal property and landholdings was taken in code form, it proved impossible to use the Lorenz Curve to illustrate inequality.

57. See Robert Brenner, "Agrarian Class Structure and Economic Development in Pre-Industrial Europe," *Past and Present* 70 (1976): 30–75, where the author develops the argument that the growth of a petty proprietorship guaranteed economic backwardness in early modern France.

NOTES TO CHAPTER II

1. Genovese, *Roll, Jordon.* Genovese argued that the destruction of slavery meant the end of paternalism as "the reigning southern ideal of social relations," but "it did not mean the total disappearance of paternalism as an ingredient in social relations" (661). Others have alleged the continuation of paternalism; however, they have not related it to the social structure. See W. J. Cash, *The Mind of the South* (New York: Vintage, 1941), 113. Woodward, *Origins,* 209, 215, 218, 223. For a challenge to Genovese's claim regarding paternalism under slavery, see Paul D. Escott, *Slavery Remembered: A Record of Twentieth-Century Slave Narratives* (Chapel Hill: Univ. of North Carolina Press, 1979), ch. 1; Edward Magdol, "Against the Gentry: An Inquiry into Southern Lower-Class Community and Culture, 1865–1870," pp. 191–210; and Vernon Burton, "Race and Reconstruction: Edgefield County, South Carolina," 211–37, both in Edward Magdol and Jon L. Wakelyn, eds. *The Southern Common People: Studies in Nineteenth-Century Social History* (Westport, Conn.: Greenwood, 1980).

2. The term "patronage" is largely a heuristic device and a form of argumentative shorthand. It is used to distinguish work relationships after the Civil War from paternalism before the war. Certainly, they were not the same. Moreover, it is used to qualify southern capitalism, which was not at all like northern free-labor capitalism, yet the

South retained essentially a capitalist economy. Patronage also describes the nature of Louisa politics, which after all flowed out of the economic structure. More importantly, the term "patronage" characterizes social relationships which have prevailed in the region for generations and generally go by the names of "manners," "gentility," and other related terms. In this form, patronage describes a kind of utilitarian deference (not to be confused with respect) powerless clients are expected to confer upon economic and political patrons to get what they need or want. Since the South has a long tradition of race and class divisions, patronage has become a well-developed art which outsiders often confuse with manners. More often, southerners are not more mannerly than other Americans, just more patronizing. Hence, I use the term "patronage" to characterize the entire range of economic, political, and social relationships and to analyze what lay behind its practice.

3. See pp. xii–xiii above for a more detailed development of these summary statements.

4. General Order No. 77, 23 June 1865, Records of the Field Offices of the Bureau of Refugees, Freemen, and Abandoned Lands, Records Group 105, National Archives and Records Service (hereafter referred to as FBR). The italics are mine.

5. Circular No. 11, 12 July 1865, FBR.

6. Circular [no number], 19 Sept. 1865, FBR.

7. Monthly Report, Louisa County, July 1866, FBR.

8. Circular [no number], 4 Nov. 1865, FBR.

9. Willie Lee Rose, *Rehearsal for Reconstruction: The Port Royal Experiment* (New York: Vintage, 1964); Wharton, *The Negro in Mississippi;* Ross, "Freed Soil," 213–32.

10. Roark, *Masters,* 138–39.

11. *Acts of the General Assembly of the State of Virginia Passed in 1865–66* (Richmond, Va., 1866), 91 (hereafter referred to as *Acts* and the date). For a discussion of the transition from a paternalistic to a more legalistic social order and the "crisis" this posed for eighteenth-century England, see E. P. Thompson, "Patrician Society, Plebian Culture," *Journal of Social History* 7 (Summer 1974): 383–405.

12. *Acts* 1866.

13. *Ibid.*

14. *Ibid.* These penalties were temporarily suspended during the Reconstruction but reinstituted again in 1887 by an act of the General Assembly. See Harriet Tynes, "History of Poor Relief Legislation in Virginia" (M.A. thesis, Univ. of Chicago, 1932), 80–82.

15. *Acts,* 1865–66, pp.83, 187. Both acts were repealed in 1871; see *Acts,* 1870–71, ch. 89, p. 147.

16. *Acts,* 1865–66, p. 201.

17. *Ibid.,* 81–82.

18. Order of Louisa County Justice of Peace, 18 Dec. 1865. Letter of Louisa Court Officer to District Office of the Freedmen's Bureau [n.d.], FBR. It is not surprising that the action occurred at Christmas, for this had been the traditional "settling up time" during slavery when slaves were given a few more freedoms, extra rations, even a little whiskey. This always made slaveowners nervous, and this anxiety may have heightened after the war when freedmen had guns. Such anxiety is documented in Dan T. Carter, "The Anatomy of Fear: The Christmas Day Insurrection Scare of 1865," *Journal of Southern History* 17, no. 3 (Aug. 1976): 345–64.

19. Wiener, "Class Structure," 982.

20. MS Labor Contract, FBR.

21. MS Labor Contract, 20 May 1865, FBR.

22. MS Contract, 27 May 1865, FBR.

23. Diary and MS Labor Contract, 5 June 1865, in the Thomas Watson Papers, Alderman Library, Univ. of Virginia.

24. MS Labor Contract, June 1865, between Eliza Shelton and Thomas Watson, Watson Papers.

25. See Genovese, *Roll, Jordon,* 450–58; John W. Blassingame, *The Slave Community* (New York: Oxford Univ. Press, 1973), 77–103; Herbert G. Gutman, *The Black Family in Slavery and Freedom 1750–1925* (New York: Random, 1977); Crandall A. Shifflett, "Household Composition of Rural Black Families: Louisa County, Virginia, 1880," *Journal of Interdisciplinary History* 6, no. 2 (Autumn 1975): 235–60; Elizabeth H. Pleck, "The Two Parent Household: Black Family Structure in Late Nineteenth Century Boston," *Journal of Social History* 6 (Fall 1972): 3–31; Peter Kolchin, *First Freedom: The Responses of Alabama's Blacks to Emancipation and Reconstruction* (Westport, Conn.: Greenwood, 1972), 56–78; and ch. 6, herein.

26. MS Labor Contract, 4 July 1865, between Watson and Harry Quarles, Watson Papers.

27. MS Labor Contract, Jan. 1866, between Jacob Ragland and Watson, *ibid.*

28. MS Labor Contract, 26 June 1865, between same Quarles and Watson, *ibid.*

29. MS Labor Contracts, Watson and John Armstead Turner, 1867; Watson and Lewis Ragland and Peter Holmes, Jan. 1867; Watson and Nat Ragland, 1868; Watson and Archy Carter, 1868; Letter, Thomas Watson to V. H. Robertson, 6 Jan. 1869, *ibid.*

30. MS Labor Contract between W. J. Winston and Luther Hughes, 12 Jan. 1866, FBR.

31. Monthly Report, Louisa County, Aug. 1866, FBR.

32. Monthly Report, Culpeper County, 31 Jan. 1868, FBR.

33. Monthly Report, Goochland County, Dec. 1867, FBR.
34. Letter David Magruder to Thomas Watson, 20 Apr. 1866, Watson Papers.
35. Letters Thomas Watson to V. H. Robertson, Nov. 1866, 28 Dec. 1866, *ibid.* Annual contracting was equally undesirable in the cotton South, where farmers liked it as a method of insuring hands for the fields but disliked it because it did not give them as complete a control over labor as slavery. The only reason they did not abandon it was because the current return to them through sharecropping was equivalent to any alternative. Unlike the cotton South, Louisa's farmers found an alternative. See Ransom and Sutch, *One Kind,* 98–103.
36. Altogether, 123 deeds were found on members of the "farmer" population sample of 1880. See Appendix.
37. *Acts,* 1872–73, entitled "An Act to Secure Advances for Agricultural Purposes," passed 2 Apr. 1873.
38. The Homestead Exemption was written into the constitution in 1867–68 when Virginia was still under the control of Republican Reconstruction. It was amended in 1869–70 as political control of the state began to slip back into the hands of white Conservatives; the amendment required a trip to the courthouse to record the exemption. *Code of Virginia Including Legislation to January 1, 1874,* prepared by George W. Mumford (1873), 98–99; *Acts,* 1869–70, pp. 198–203.
39. Homestead exemptions as a percentage of all instruments recorded in Louisa deedbooks in the years which I counted and classified the various types of instruments (1872, 1875, 1880, 1885, 1890, and 1900) never exceeded 4 percent of the total; in the peak year of 1880, 21 persons claimed this benefit. See *Index of Deeds, Louisa County, Grantors, 1872–1904.* Moreover, the provision was ultimately declared unconstitutional by the federal Supreme Court; see Allen W. Moger, *Virginia: Bourbonism to Byrd, 1870–1925* (Charlottesville: Univ. Press of Virginia, 1968), 77.
40. MS Deed, in Louisa Deedbook, Grantors, 2: 179, 27 Nov. 1874 (hereafter referred to as LDB). Race and occupational status were derived from the 1880 Manuscript Census of Population and Landbooks of Louisa County.
41. MS Deed, LDB, 1: 318.
42. MS Deed, LDB, 11: 583–84.
43. MS Deed, LDB, 21: 427–28.
44. MS Deed, LDB, 2: 330.
45. *Index of Deeds, 1872–1904.* In 1880 and 1900, debt instruments as a percentage of total instruments are 31 and 32 percent, respectively.

46. Thomas Watson to Mrs. John R. Robertson, Demopolis, Ala. 6 Jan. 1880, Watson Papers. Watson's records reveal a definite casualness about labor arrangements beginning about 1870. Wage rates and terms of hiring are sometimes scrawled on shreds of paper and one cannot be certain of the nature of the agreements. What is evident is that Watson moves away from long-term rentals to more and more day labor and to fewer total laborers as he follows the trend of others toward grass farming and livestock raising; see ch. 4.

47. This is a model proposed by Eric Wolf to analyze peasant coalitions which suggests the potential importance of encumbering alliances to the social order. See Eric R. Wolf, *Peasants* (Englewood Cliffs, N.J.: Prentice-Hall, 1966), esp. 60–95; Wolf, "Kinship, Friendship, and Patron-Client Relations in Complex Societies," in Michael Banton, ed., *The Social Anthropology of Complex Societies* (London: Tavistock, 1968), 1–22. See also Marshal Sahlins, "On the Sociology of Primitive Exchange," in Michael Banton, ed., *The Relevance of Models for Social Anthropology* (London: Tavistock, 1968), 139–86. For other studies which make use of the model of vertical and horizontal relations, see Allen Johnson, *Sharecroppers of the Sertão* and Julian A. Pitt-Rivers, *The People of the Sierra*.

48. See ch. 6 for a discussion of the political dimension of patronage and ch. 3, pp. 50–51, for evidence of political manipulation of clients.

49. See p. 35, above.

50. See ch. 4.

51. See ch. 4.

NOTES TO CHAPTER III

1. See Appendix for a more detailed discussion of the sample population.

2. The gauge for this calculation was those who paid $2 or less in personal property taxes in 1880. Another study found 90 percent of the black and 54 percent of the white population in the same circumstances; see Orville Vernon Burton, "Ungrateful Servants? Edgefield's Black Reconstruction: Part I of the Total History of Edgefield County, South Carolina" (Ph.D. diss., Princeton Univ., 1975), 237–43. As for the sample's being representative of the entire population, it is probably skewed, but in the direction of underrepresenting the poor. Certainly a sample of those who listed their occupation as "farmer" would include more of the wealthy. See Appendix for a discussion of methodology.

3. Eugene D. Genovese, "The Legacy of Slavery and the Roots of Black Nationalism (Revised)," in Genovese, *In Red and Black: Marxian Explorations in Southern and Afro-American History* (New York: Vintage, 1971), 129–57.

4. The biographies of laborers and renters have been compiled by linking the following sources: MS Censuses of Population and Agriculture, 1870 and 1880; Louisa personal property and land tax records, 1870, 1880, 1890 and 1900.

5. These averages were gained from personal property taxbooks for 1880 by dividing the total number of animals in the county by their total assessed value.

6. MS Census, Social Statistics, 1870.

7. *State Agricultural Report, 1877,* p. 49. Louisa, however, was representative of the South, where wage rates for laborers were below those of the rest of the United States. See Woodward, *Origins,* 207. See also, Carl Kelsey, *The Negro Farmer* (Chicago: Jennings and Pye, 1903); William T. Thom, *The Negroes of Sandy Spring, Maryland: A Social Study,* Bulletin No. 32 (U. S. Department of Labor, 1901), 43–102; and W. E. B. DuBois, *The Negro in the Black Belt: Some Social Sketches,* Bulletin No. 22 (U.S. Department of Labor, 1899), 401–17.

8. *State Agricultural Report, 1877,* p. 49.

9. *State Agricultural Report, 1893,* pp. 76–77.

10. W. E. B. DuBois, *The Negroes of Farmville, Virginia,* Bulletin No. 14 (U. S. Department of Labor, 1898), 28–29. DuBois found 19 percent of the families making less than enough to cover expenses and about 50 percent earning the minimum. Another study of 19 black families in Tidewater Virginia found the average cost of food per adult per day to be 11¢. If one allows a full 11¢ for two adults and one-half of that for each three children, the food costs for a family of five would be about 50¢ per day or $3.50 per week, about double what DuBois found. Again, the food portion of household expenses must have varied, depending upon household produce and perhaps other factors such as caloric needs for different labor tasks. At any rate, DuBois's average of $220 in expenses for a family of five seems reasonable. Farmville, Va., is the county seat of Prince Edward County. Like Louisa, Prince Edward County is in the central Virginia Piedmont and was once a county dominated by slaveholding tobacco farmers. See also Hollis B. Frissell and Isabel Beviar, *Dietary Studies of Negroes in Eastern Virginia in 1897 and 1898,* Experiment Station Bulletin No. 71 (U. S. Department of Labor, 1899). A study of 5,600 farm laborers in Michigan's lower peninsula in 1894 found average monthly wages of $18, double that of Louisa in the same year, and yet just over 50 percent said this was

enough to support their families. See Michigan Bureau of Labor and Industrial Statistics, *Twelfth Annual Report,* pt. 1 (1895), 1–236.

11. The number of families for 1870 and 1880 was not available in the general census tables by county. It was derived by totaling family numbers used by the census takers and noted on the manuscript schedules for these years. For 1890 and 1900, see *Twelfth Census, 1900: Population,* II: 638.

12. No record existed of the numbers of deaths by starvation, but evidence of starvation is presented in ch. 5.

13. General Ledger, Charles Danne's Store, Manuscript Division, Alderman Library, University of Virginia.

14. Freedmen's Bureau records occasionally noted stills in nearby Madison County, but I found no references to them in Louisa.

15. See n. 4, above, for the source of biographical information.

16. Renters are those whose occupation is described as tenants or sharecroppers on the 1880 MS Census of Agriculture and who local landbooks revealed owned no land in Louisa.

17. 1880 MS Census of Agriculture.

18. *Ibid.*

19. Based upon percentage of acreage devoted to each crop, as revealed in *ibid.*

20. Based upon the most frequently listed animals in *ibid.*

21. See ch. 6 for a detailed examination of the relationship between household and economy. See Gutman, *The Black Family,* 443, and n. 7, pp. 628–32, for evidence that black women worked in the fields.

22. Monthly Report, Louisa County, 28 Feb. 1866, FBR.

23. Monthly Report, Lynchburg, 28 Feb. 1866, FBR.

24. It has been shown that in the cotton South during the Emancipation Period the black population actually may have withheld its labor as the supply of black agricultural labor dropped as low as two-thirds of slave labor levels. Ransom and Sutch, *One Kind,* 44–47, 232–36.

25. Monthly Reports, Lynchburg, Feb. 1866 and Jan. 1867; Richmond, Apr. 1867; Norfolk, Feb. 1867; and Charlottesville, Jan. 1866, all FBR.

26. Isabella Burnet, Louisa County History Scrapbook, (manuscript, Rare Books, University of Virginia Library).

27. Arthur G. Peterson, *Historical Study of Prices Received by Producers of Farm Products in Virginia,* Bulletin No. 37 (Blacksburg, Va.: Virginia Polytechnic Institute, Mar. 1929), 16; Gates, *The Farmer's Age,* 104.

28. Monthly Report, Richmond, Mar. 1866, FBR.

29. Monthly Report, Richmond, Apr. 1867; Lynchburg, Feb. 1866, FBR. Wages in Richmond and Lynchburg tobacco factories ranged from $10 to $15 per month.

30. Letter, Thomas Watson to V. H. Robertson, 15 Aug. 1868, Watson Papers.

31. Everett S. Lee, et al., *Population Redistribution and Economic Growth, United States 1870–1950* (Philadelphia: American Philosophical Society, 1957), I: 293.

32. Monthly Report, Louisa County, Feb. 1867, FBR.

33. Monthly Report, Louisa County, 31 Aug. 1867; Madison County, 31 May 1868, FBR.

34. Monthly Report, Louisa County, July and Aug. 1866, FBR.

35. See, for example, the contract of Horace Jefferson and Watson, 1 July 1865, Watson Papers.

36. MS Contract, 2 Apr. 1866, between Baptist Trustees and John Chiles, FBR. Actually, the church was turned into a Freedmen's school, which did not violate the contract, and local whites and blacks held a fair in the church to raise money for the school. Monthly Report, 31 Aug. 1866, FBR.

37. Monthly Report, Madison County, 31 Aug. 1867, FBR.

38. Monthly Report, Louisa County, 31 Oct. 1867, FBR.

39. Monthly Reports, Madison County, 31 May 1868; Culpeper County, May 1868; Goochland County, May 1868, FBR.

40. Letter of Thomas Watson to V. H. Robertson, July 1868, Watson Papers.

41. *Ibid.*

42. Monthly Report, Charlottesville, July 1867, FBR. The city of Charlottesville is located about 35 miles from Louisa Courthouse in Albermarle County.

43. List of Felons or Other Infamous Offenses in Louisa County, Virginia Since November 2nd, 1870, Louisa Courthouse. It is not clear whether this is a complete record of felonious crime or merely a list of unsolved crimes. Since no other index of crime could be found, a thorough reading of all the court cases in the county would be required to answer the questions about the extent of this form of resistance.

44. Virginius Dabney, *Virginia: The New Dominion; A History from 1607 to the Present* (Garden City, N. Y.: Doubleday, 1971), ·420.

45. *Ibid.*

46. Woodward, *Origins,* 245; William DuBose Sheldon, *Populism in the Old Dominion, Virginia Farm Politics, 1885–1900* (Princeton: Princeton Univ. Press, 1935), 25–35, 45, 95–96.

47. Robert C. McMath, Jr., *Populist Vanguard: A History of the Southern Farmers' Alliance* (Chapel Hill: Univ. of North Carolina Press, 1975), 153.

48. Dabney, *Virginia*, 423.

49. Lee, *Population Redistribution*, I: 343.

50. The actual number of blacks enumerated in Louisa was 10,063 in 1870, 11,531 in 1880, 9,805 in 1890, and 8,621 in 1900; and whites: 6,269 in 1870, 7,409 in 1880, 7,192 in 1890, and 7,896 in 1900. The increase of the black population in 1870 may be spurious due to the widely acknowledged underenumeration of the black population. The Census Bureau estimated the undercount to be 9.5 percent in 1870. Using this estimate for Louisa, one could add about 1,000 to the black population for 1870, bringing the number of blacks in that year to 11,063. The revised figure suggests that the migration was heaviest after 1880. For the estimate of the undercount, see *Compendium of the Eleventh Census: 1890*, pt. I, pp. xxxv–xliii. Regarding the undercount, see *Compendium of the Tenth Census (June 1, 1880)*, liv–lxxvi; Francis A. Walker, "Statistics of the Colored Race in the United States," in *Publications of the American Statistical Association*, n.s. 2 (Sept. and Dec. 1890): 91–106. Ransom and Sutch have tried to refine the estimates in "The Impact of the Civil War and of Emancipation on Southern Agriculture," in *Explorations in Economic History* 12 (Jan. 1975): 1–28.

51. Unlike the "farmer" sample, this was a totally random sample of every tenth person on the census; see Appendix.

52. The actual number of black owners was 22 in 1870 out of 1,357 landowners, 199 out of 1,872 in 1880, and 1,314 out of 3,337 in 1900. These figures came from the Louisa landbooks for 1870, 1880, and 1900. Gains in black landholdings were not confined to poor counties like Louisa. Blacks owned only 500 acres in 24 counties of the Tidewater region after the war, but by 1912 they owned 421,465 acres. In Prince Edward County, a tobacco county of the Virginia Piedmont, blacks owned 13 percent of the land by 1906. T. C. Walker, "Development in the Tidewater Counties of Virginia," *The Annals of the American Academy of Political and Social Science* 49 (Sept. 1913), 28–31; W. T. B. Williams, "Local Conditions Among Negroes, III, Prince Edward County, Virginia," *Southern Workman* 35 (April 1906), 239–44.

53. Thomas J. Watson to Mrs. John R. Robertson, 28 Jan. 1884, Watson Papers.

54. Lewis Ragland to Thomas J. Watson, 5 Oct. 1884, 13 Nov. 1884, and 16 Aug. 1892, all in Watson Papers.

55. Receipt on account of Shadrack Johnson, 26 Oct. 1887, *ibid.*
56. Agreement between Holmes, Ragland, and Watson, 1 Apr. 1887, *ibid.*
57. Hugh H. Bennett and W. E. McLendon, "Soil Survey of Louisa County Virginia," *Field Operations of the Bureau of Soils, 1905* (Washington, D. C.: Department of Agriculture, 7th Report, 1907), 191–92. For an example of a black owner who also rented, see the case of William Mitchell, ch. 1, pp. 21–22. It is impossible to determine the frequency of owner-renters, but as Mitchell's case illustrates, the owners of these patches could be just as desperate as nonowner renters.
58. C. Vann Woodward, *The Strange Career of Jim Crow* (New York: Oxford Univ. Press, 1974).
59. Charles E. Wynes, *Race Relations in Virginia, 1870–1902* (Charlottesville, Va.: Univ. Press of Virginia, 1961).
60. Edmund S. Morgan, *American slavery, American Freedom: The Ordeal of Colonial Virginia* (New York: Norton, 1975), ch. 16; Genovese, *Roll, Jordon,* 285, 295, 298, 304–5, and 309; and George M. Frederickson, *The Black Image in the White Mind: The Debate on Afro-American Character and Destiny, 1817–1914* (New York: Harper and Row 1971), esp. the sections on paternalistic racism.
61. *First Annual Report of the Commissioner of Agriculture in Virginia, 1877* (Richmond, Va., 1877), 48–49.
62. *Annual Report of Agriculture in Virginia, 1879* (Richmond, Va., 1879), 131.
63. Mrs. V. M. Watson (Barker), Clarksville, Tenn., to Mrs. Thomas S. Watson, 6 Apr. 1884, Watson Papers.
64. Quoted in Woodward, *Origins,* 53.

NOTES TO CHAPTER IV

1. A study of Louisiana farmers between 1840 and 1875 found the 100-acre farm to be the limit of the family farm and referred to those over 100 acres as "plantations." See Roger W. Shugg, *Origins,* p. 7n. The Virginia Bureau of Agriculture also noted that a family of six could supply enough labor for a 100-acre farm. See *Virginia Annual Report of Agriculture, 1893* (Richmond, Va.), 29–35. See also Bennett and McLendon, "Soil Survey," 211. The same sources noted that from one-third to one-half of the land in any given year was normally fallowed.
2. Sample population, 1880 Manuscript Census of Population. For determination of farm tenure, see Appendix.

3. Thomas S. Watson to James Smith, 27 Feb. 1869, Watson Papers.

4. Virginia Watson to Thomas S. Watson, Jr. at Virginia Military Institute, 21 Apr. 1876, *ibid.*

5. Letter, Thomas Watson to John R. Robertson, 8 Dec. 1880, *ibid.*

6. Letter, Thomas Watson to V. H. Robertson, 12 Nov. 1880, *ibid.*

7. Letter, Thomas Watson to V. H. Robertson, Mar. 1881, *ibid.*

8. Letters Thomas S. Watson to John R. Robertson, 4 Jan. 1884; H. M. Magruder to Thomas S. Watson, 20 Feb. 1884; James Holladay to Thomas S. Watson, 28 Feb. 1884; Bill of Sale for wool and eggs; all in *ibid.*

9. *Virginia Annual Report on Agriculture, 1895.* The report described cattle business in Virginia as "quite active" and noted that poultry had shown a great increase.

10. See Appendix.

11. 1880 Manuscript Census of Agriculture.

12. *Virginia Annual Report of Agriculture, 1880,* pp. 14–21.

13. *Ibid, 1887,* p. 61.

14. Woodward, *Origins,* 129–30. See also Shannon, *The Farmer's Last Frontier,* 117–20; Nannie May Tilly, *The Bright Tobacco Industry, 1860–1929* (Chapel Hill: Univ. of North Carolina Press, 1948).

15. Manuscript Census of Agriculture, 1880; Louisa Landbook, 1870 and 1880.

16. Manuscript Census of Agriculture, 1870 and 1880.

17. *Virginia Annual Report of Agriculture, 1895,* p. 23.

18. Thomas S. Watson to Mrs. John R. Robertson, 4 Jan. 1884, Watson Papers.

19. Unlike these tobacco counties, the cotton South became more dependent upon cash crops after the war. See Ransom and Sutch, *One Kind,* 102–3.

20. *Virginia Annual Report of Agriculture, 1887,* pp. 4–9.

21. *Ibid., 1889,* p. 19.

22. *Ibid.* See also *ibid., 1891,* p. 18, and *1899,* p. 6.

23. *Ibid., 1893,* p. 62.

24. *Ibid., 1895,* p. 22.

25. Letters Thomas Watson to V. H. Robertson, 10 Feb. 1880, Robert Beverley to Thomas S. Watson, Jr., May 1880, Watson Papers. These comments point out the difficulty of measuring the extent of wealth and its concentration in the South generally. Watson might have had holdings in still other counties and states, and other largeholders in Louisa County, like Watson, probably had more extensive holdings than county records indicate. County lines

are artificial boundaries. However, I do not wish to make an argument against local studies so much as to make a plea that more be done; see also Appendix.

26. Thomas S. Watson to Mrs. John R. Robertson, 4 Jan. 1884, Watson Papers.

27. *Virginia Annual Report of Agriculture, 1899,* p. 6.

28. Prices quoted here are taken from Peterson, "Historical Study of Prices," 1–218. His prices are the average prices of farm products received by producers each month, as collected from records or original sales. My quotations are annual averages of Peterson's monthly averages. Louisa County store ledgers and plantation records also confirm the same trend. See also, Shannon, *The Farmer's Last Frontier,* 291–328. Shannon noted that prices for manufactured goods were also depressed, though not as much as farm commodity prices, and farmers also managed to hold wages steady. Hence, in real dollars, the depression in agriculture was not as catastrophic as these prices suggest. Indeed, areas of the Midwest experienced solid agricultural growth. The South had other problems, however, that when combined with depressed farm prices made the depression more intense in the South. New pressures such as labor costs, depleted soil that required application of increasing amounts of expensive fertilizer, concentrated wealth, and the loss of the South's competitive advantage in wheat growing are problems midwestern agriculture did not face. For evidence of the South's use of "prodigious quantities" of fertilizer and the negative results of concentrated wealth on the macro level, see Ransom and Sutch, *One Kind,* 80, 102–3. For evidence of the loss of self-sufficiency in the South as a whole, its dependence upon cash crops, and regional specialization, see Ransom and Sutch, *ibid.,* 151–59; Douglass C. North, *The Economic Growth of the United States, 1790–1860* (New York: Norton, 1966).

29. 1880 Manuscript Census of Agriculture.

30. *Virginia Annual Report of Agriculture, 1883,* p. 19.

31. Letter, James Rawlings to Thomas Watson, 13 Aug. 1869, Watson Papers.

32. Letter, Thomas Watson to V. H. Robertson, March 1881, *ibid.*

33. Louisa Landbook, 1863 and 1899. In number, 25 middling and 21 large farmers showed decreases.

34. Thomas S. Watson, Jr., to Mrs. V. H. Robertson, 14 Mar. 1884, Watson Papers.

35. Wiener, "Class Structure," 985–86.

36. See ch. 1, p. 8.

37. Harold D. Woodman, "Sequel to Slavery: The New History Views the Postbellum South," *Journal of Southern History* 43, no. 4 (Nov. 1977): 554. Although I disagree with Woodman's implication that capitalism evolved in the South after the war, I agree wholeheartedly with his larger point that the market "is a product of the society in which it exists," that it is "a political and social as well as an economic institution" (534). Indeed, this study of Louisa is based upon this presupposition. The next chapter develops this point further.

38. Agreement of Thomas S. Watson with Thomas S. Watson, Jr., 15 Oct. 1890; letters Henry J. Wale to Thomas S. Watson, 10 and 11 Sept. 1884; Thomas S. Watson to Ellen, 12 June 1896; all in Watson Papers.

39. Thomas S. Watson, Jr., to Mrs. V. H. Robertson, 14 Mar. 1884, *ibid.* Such preoccupation with wealth and status continues, of course. Recently, the local newspaper ran a series on "Old Homes of Louisa." All of the sketches and pictures were of ancestral homes of old plantation families. No dwellings of nonslaveholding whites were included and no slave cabins. Two very old former slaves were featured. Charlie Robinson, a former slave of Watson's, is quoted recalling slavery as "The happiest days of my life." Yet, for the remainder of the sketch, he talks about the white slave patrols, their cruelty, and the whip lashings he received for leaving the plantation at night. In detail, he describes being brought to a room with a metal ring in the floor where he was forced to kneel and receive his beatings. The local newspaper editor refused to give me the photographer's name, until pressed, because "she had no authority" to release information to me on these homes and families.

40. Letter, Thomas Watson to V. H. Robertson, 6 Jan. 1869, Watson Papers.

41. *Virginia Annual Report of Agriculture, 1889,* p. 24.

NOTES TO CHAPTER V

1. Woodman, "Sequel," 534.
2. Thomas Watson to Mrs. V. H. Robertson, 15 Oct. 1868, Watson Papers.
3. Roark, *Masters,* 180.
4. *Ibid.,* 181.
5. Rhys Issac has argued that the courthouse was "a focal point of the most intense social significance" in the revolutionary period in Virginia, whose society he characterized as a "face-to-face society." His characterization seems to fit this later period as well. More than

NOTES TO PAGES 68-71

its bricks and mortar, courthouse actions, whether the official recording of transactions, the dispensing of small favors, or the meting
out of penalties, legitimated the forms of wealth and power embedded in a structure of economic inequality. See Rhys Issac, "Drama-
tizing the Ideology of Revolution: Popular Mobilization in Virginia,
1774 to 1776," *William and Mary Quarterly* 33, no. 3 (July 1976): esp.
358–61 and 364–67.

6. In 1895 the Board of Supervisors decided against building a
new courthouse "in view of the fact that our people are struggling
under the general financial depression and unable in many instances
to pay the present rate of taxation." In 1902 the board asked the state
legislature for permission to issue bonds up to $10,000 to pay for the
erection of a new courthouse, county offices, and enclosing of the
property. In 1903, $400 was appropriated for the Confederate
monument. Louisa Board of Supervisor's Journal (2 vols.), 2: 266,
294 (hereafter referred to as BOS Journal with volume and page
numbers).

7. Local ordinances and decrees of the Board of Supervisors
required these postings.

8. Arthur W. James, *The Disappearance of the County Almshouse in
Virginia* (Richmond: State Department of Public Welfare, 1926),
5–7; Joseph Cepuran, *Public Assistance and Child Welfare: The Virginia Pattern, 1646 to 1964* (Charlottesville: Institute of Government,
Univ. of Virginia, 1968), 8–37; Robert H. Kirkwood, *Fit Surroundings: District Homes Replace County Almshouses in Virginia* (Richmond: Virginia Department of Public Welfare, 1948), 20–23; Frank
William Hoffer, *Counties in Transition: A Study of County Public and
Private Welfare Administration in Virginia* (Charlottesville: The Institute of Research in Social Sciences, Univ. of Virginia, 1929), 47–69;
Harriet L. Tynes, "History of Poor Relief Legislation in Virginia,"
(M.A. thesis, Univ. of Chicago, 1932), 12. As these sources point
out, the colonists borrowed heavily upon English poor laws and
experience for their solutions to poverty.

9. James, *The Disappearance,* 7–8. Also, see my map on p. 10 for
the location of the poorhouse.

10. Hoffer, *Counties,* 47–91; Cepuran, *History,* 8–37; Kirkwood,
Fit Surroundings, 20–23. The vestry was a powerful institution in
eighteenth-century Virginia "which served as an immediate embodi-
ment of social authority both secular and religious." Rhys Issac,
"Religion and Authority: Problems of the Anglican Establishment in
Virginia in the Era of the Great Awakening and the Parsons' Cause,"
William and Mary Quarterly 30, no. 1 (Jan. 1973): 6.

11. Kirkwood, *Fit Surroundings,* 24; Cepuran, *History,* 8–37;
Hoffer, *Counties,* 51, 70–91.

12. BOS Journal, 2: 211.

13. Hoffer, *Counties,* 70–91.

14. *First Annual Report of the State Board of Charities and Corrections* (Richmond, Va.: Superintendent of Public Printing, 1909), 39. The establishment of this board was the result of the work of citizen reform groups who became concerned about conditions in the alms-houses. North Carolina was the first southern state to sanction state action to reform the almshouse by establishing its board in 1869. Nearly forty years passed before the Virginia bureaucracy could be persuaded to take similar steps. The Virginia Conference of Charity and Corrections was formed in 1900 to lobby for state action. It took four years to convince the governor that he should recommend state action to the General Assembly. Another four years passed before the State Board of Charities and Corrections was organized in 1907. Their report describes every almshouse in the state and the almost unspeakable conditions they found. Old men and women lived in filthy rooms, some dying alone with no one to care for them. One almshouse housed 19 "inmates" in five cottage rooms. Victims of tuberculosis slept in the same rooms with the healthy. One superintendent had nailed shut the windows of his cottages to keep residents from leaving without his permission. In another instance, inspectors found a 21-year-old girl who carried a ball and chain during the day weighing 28 pounds to keep her from wandering away. The superintendent explained he did not have time to look after her and he could not afford anyone to watch her. When the state board reported this, the girl was declared insane and transferred to a state hospital. In fact, the board found very few able-bodied poor in any workhouse at the time of its inspection.

15. The same move away from rehabilitation toward custodial care was true for other institutions as well, such as the asylum and the penitentiary. See David J. Rothman, *The Discovery of the Asylum* (Boston: Little, Brown, 1971).

16. Hoffer, *Counties,* 47–67.

17. Monthly Report, Goochland County, 20 Nov. 1868, FBR.

18. General Order No. 20, 16 Sept. 1865, FBR.

19. Order signed by Capt. Cramden, District Superintendent, 6 July 1865, FBR.

20. Circular Letter, 4 Oct. 1865, FBR. In monthly reports there is also evidence that bureau officials believed that poverty was a result of character weaknesses, relief should be given sparingly, and "dependency" should be guarded against. These, as I have noted, were common attitudes toward poverty during the nineteenth century. See Robert H. Bremner, *From the Depths: The Discovery of Poverty in the United States* (New York: New York Univ. Press, 1969).

21. Monthly Reports, Orange County, 2 Apr. 1865; Fluvanna County, 9 Apr. 1866; Culpeper County, Apr. 1866; Giles County, 12 Apr. 1866; Princess Anne County, Aug. 1865; Essex County, 27 Apr. 1866, FBR.

22. Monthly Report, Louisa County, Apr. 1866, FBR.

23. Monthly Reports, 24 May 1866 and Oct. 1866, Louisa County, FBR.

24. BOS Journal, 1: 24–39. Figures are rounded to the nearest dollar. The county actually collected more than this, as we saw in ch. 2, but in this chapter we are concerned with the collections and disbursements for county purposes. Additional funds were also paid to the state.

25. BOS Journal, 1: 64.

26. See ch. 2, p. 27.

27. See n. 47, below.

28. BOS Journal, 1: 211–35, 314–41; 2: 40–64, 133–54, 258–69.

29. *Ibid.,* 1: 187, 199; 2: 138.

30. *Ibid.,* 1: 192.

31. *Ibid.,* 355–56. Unfortunately, these valuable lists could not be located in the courthouse, although they had been compiled, as later entries show.

32. *Ibid.,* 89, 175, 375.

33. Annual Report of the Auditor of Public Accounts of the Commonwealth of Virginia, Louisa County, 1876, 1880, and 1881 (unpublished reports located at the Virginia State Library).

34. BOS Journal, 1: 246, 355–56, 360, 375; 2: 12, 53, 102. The county also reimbursed patrons for transporting paupers to the almshouse, hiring a team of horses, and buying food.

35. BOS Journal, 2: 233.

36. Based upon a general statement showing the aggregate amount of receipts and expenditures located in loose form in the BOS Journal, vol. 2. The remainder of the budget for fiscal year 1899 included 6 percent for political expenses, 5 percent for dealing with smallpox, 5 percent for indexing county records (required by a new state law), and 12 percent on delinquent taxes and other debts.

37. The source of data for these figures are the land and personal propety taxbooks for the years indicated, which list the holdings and tax payments of each person in the county. The landbooks list the number of acres, value of the land per acre, value of buildings, and the tax assessed. Personal property books list the number of horses, cattle, sheep, carriages, pianos, gold and silverplate, watches, clocks, sewing machines, and their values; the value of household and kitchen furniture; amount of income over $600 (the taxable

amount); the amount of holdings in bonds, notes, and securities; and the tax paid on all personal property.

38. See ch. 1, pp. 9, 15–16.

39. Based upon the 1880 "farmer" sample. Among whites who paid personal property taxes, 134 of 227 paid $2 or less; among blacks, 199 of 200.

40. These collective biographies were composed by locating the county leaders in the following records: PP. Book, 1863; Louisa Landbook, 1876. The list of leaders was found in one of the few extant editions of a contemporary newspaper, *Louisa Weekly Record,* 3 June 1876. Changes in positions held by the leaders were found in *Louisa County News,* 9 Dec. 1898, and in various references in the BOS Journal. The records did not permit a detailed tracing of the positions these leaders may have held in other years, but even these scattered sources reveal a rotation of the same elite in and out of various county offices.

41. Jack P. Maddex, Jr., *The Virginia Conservatives, 1867–1879: A Study in Reconstruction Politics* (Chapel Hill: Univ. of North Carolina Press, 1970), 12, 173–75. Maddex sees the changes uprooting the "old ancient squirearchy" (175), but this was not the case at all in Louisa.

42. Moger, *Virginia,* 97.

43. BOS Journal, 1: 390. Actually, Louisa had a fourth district—Louisa Courthouse—but this district's registration was missing. No other voter registration records could be found. For the district boundaries, see map p. 10.

44. The taxbook showed 1,503 white males, while 1,543 were registered in three districts!

45. The generalization that the political and economic elite were the primary benefactors of patronage dispensed through the county treasury is difficult to quantify precisely. One would have to know the economic, political, and racial identities of everyone in the county during this period. Yet even without the benefit of this omniscience, I can safely make the generalization on the basis of other clues. My study of individuals has familiarized me with the economic, political, and racial characteristics of large numbers of Louisans whose names I recognize immediately and whose status I am able to confirm generally. Also, Louisa blacks rarely had middle initials in their names, and payments to those recorded on the BOS Journal with middle initials were extremely rare. Finally, when payments to blacks were recorded in the journal, their racial identity was often (though not always) given. In any year of the journal record, payments to those without middle initials (whom I could not otherwise identify) and to those noted as "colored" never composed

as many as 1 percent of the recipients of money. Rather, the payments for "dividing the county into townships," "certifying elections," "surveyor," "repairs to road," "use of team on road," "repairs to bridges," "for timber," "repairs to jail," "taking paupers to poorhouse," "furnishing maps," etc., typically went to local doctors, lawyers, and landowners who could be recognized by their names alone as political leaders, recalled from my sample and identified as landowners, or who, in the case of physicians or dentists, were usually referred to as "Dr."

46. BOS Journal, 1: 248–52; 2: 102, 278.

47. Coffins for paupers were estimated at two-year intervals between 1888 and 1900. The number is "estimated" because some entries on the journal were for cumulative sums. Coffins usually cost $2 each and some entries merely note "Coffins—$6" for a three-month period. I assumed three coffins in these cases. Besides 1890–91, the next highest number was 52 in 1898, but this figure is uncertain because of the way ditto marks were used. I reduced this figure to 21 for the purposes of calculating the yearly average, and counted only those which I could definitely identify as expenses for coffins. For the other years the figures seem to be reasonable. Then average as an estimate of pauper deaths is still probably conservative, however, because not all unable to afford a coffin attempted to get burial assistance from the courthouse. Also, occasionally, entries note that only $1 was paid to a coffin builder. Finally, other entries, such as "pauper claims," may have been for coffins but were not included in estimates. The average can be taken, however, as the lowest possible number of pauper deaths per year.

NOTES TO CHAPTER VI

1. Only small numbers found work in grist and flour mills, lumber camps, mines, or on railroad crews. The 1880 Manuscript Census of Industry for Louisa County counted 91 workers in these industries.

2. Voluntary associations appeared in Virginia, created by those in need of aid at times of emergency. Two black organizations were established, the Order of Saint Luke in 1867 and the Order of the Good Samaritans in 1872, which paid sick and death benefits out of a levy on the membership. Although more research is needed on organizations like these, they do not appear to have been as widespread and effective as those of urban America. See John Marcus

Ellison, *Negro Organizations and Leadership in Relation to Rural Life in Virginia* (Blacksburg, Va., 1933).

3. See Norman E. Whitten, Jr., and John F. Szwed, "Introduction," in Whitten and Szwed, eds., *Afro-American Anthropology* (New York: Free Press, 1970), 23–53, which stresses the importance of the family under conditions of economic marginality.

4. In tables throughout this chapter, the total number of families may be less than the total number in the initial "farmer" sample. Some families had to be excluded from the analyses because data on them were missing. The "all other" category was distributed as follows:

Type of Household	% (N) Black	% (N) White
Single person	2 (5)	5 (14)
Single head with other members	4 (10)	7 (20)
Widowed heads	10 (25)	8 (24)
Nuclear family with grandchildren	7 (18)	2 (5)
Stem family (Married children living with parents)	4 (11)	2 (6)
Unable to determine	1 (2)	2 (5)

5. E. Franklin Frazier, *The Negro Family in the United States* (Chicago: Univ. of Chicago Press, 1939). Frazier did not argue that black families were predominantly woman-headed, but he emphasized the male-absent household along with other pathologies to such an extraordinary degree that he obscured a more important finding, namely, that most black families did not succumb to family disorganization. Andrew Billingsley, "The Treatment of Negro Families in American Scholarship," in *Black Families in White America* (Englewood Cliffs, N. J.: Prentice-Hall, 1966), 197–215, has noted a common tendency among students of black families to treat them as social problems.

6. For more detailed surveys of the literature, see Gutman, "Persistent Myths About the Afro-American Family," and Shifflett, "Household Composition," both in *Journal of Interdisciplinary History* 6, no. 2 (Autumn 1975). For surveys of the sociological literature, see Robert Staples, "Towards a Sociology of the Black Family: A Theoretical and Methodological Assessment," *Journal of Marriage and the Family* 33 (1971): 119–38.

7. A similar model was used by Lutz Berkner in his study of Austrian peasants. However, the life-cycle model is less likely to be distorting if it is tied to the age of the mother than if it is based on the age of the head of the household, as used by Berkner. In the former case, it is more attuned to the childbearing years of the family. It is

possible for the head of the household to be past this period in age, although this may not be a true reflection of the developmental phase of the family as a whole. This is especially true where a large age difference exists between the household head and his wife, a not uncommon situation among a number of black families. Lutz K. Berkner, "The Stem Family and the Developmental Cycle of the Peasant Household: An Eighteenth Century Austrian Example," *American Historical Review* 77, no. 2 (1972): 348–418. See also Paul C. Glick, "The Family Cycle," *American Sociological Review* 12 (1947): 164–74; Glick and Robert Parke, Jr., "New Approaches in Studying the Life Cycle of the Family," *Demography* 2 (1965): 187–202. For evidence that family structure and some measure of family age are related, see Thomas K. Burch, "Comparative Family Structure: A Demographic Approach," *Estadistica* 26 (1968): 291–93.

8. Thomas K. Burch, "Some Demographic Determinants of Average Household Size: An Analytic Approach," in Peter Laslett and Richard Wall, eds., *Household and Family in Past Time* (Cambridge: Cambridge Univ. Press, 1972), 91–102; see also *idem.* "The Size and Structure of Families: A Comparative Analysis of Census Data," *American Sociological Review* 32 (1967): 347–63.

9. A. V. Chayanov, *The Theory of Peasant Economy* ed. Daniel Thorner, Basile Kerblay, and R. E. F. Smith (Homewood, Ill.: Dorsey, 1966), 53–69. This is a brilliant theoretical treatment of the relationship between the life cycle and family structure. Chayanov divided all members of a household into either consumers or workers and then divided the number of workers into the number of consumers to get a consumer / worker ratio. He used this ratio to support his contention that family size determined farm size. He viewed peasant families as "labor machines" which sought to satisfy their consumption demands but did not strive for profit.

10. For additional evidence of racial limitations on black mobility, see 50, 54, 56, 45–47, 94–95 herein.

11. Apparently, this response of families to poverty is characteristic of the poor; see Raymond T. Smith, "The Nuclear Family in Afro-American Kinship," *Journal of Comparative Family Studies* 1 (1970): 55–70; Michael Young and Peter Willmott, *Family and Kinship in East London* (Baltimore: Penguin, 1971); and Michael Anderson, *Family Structure in Nineteenth Century Lancashire* (Cambridge: Cambridge Univ. Press, 1971).

12. Louisa Marriage Register, No. 3, 1865–1941 (hereinafter referred to as *Marriage Register*). See n. 19 below for an explanation of the sample years. In calculating these mean ages, I eliminated those marrying over age 35 and the widowed population. When these are included, the mean ages for blacks are 25.5 and 21.7 and

whites 27.4 and 23.3 for males and females, respectively. A mean of 54 white and 68 black marriages were consummated each year.

13. Typically, marriages took place in the home of the bride, regardless of race, and continued a pattern common since slavery of marriage around Christmas time. The places of marriage were located in MS Certificates of Marriage, Louisa County Courthouse, and were sampled for the years 1870, 1875, 1882, 1890, and 1900. An average of 40 percent of white marriages and 38 percent of black marriages occurred in the home of the bride for these years. The remainder took place in various other places in the county.

14. In order to be certain about the spacing of children, I had to narrow computations to those cases where the number of children ever born and children in the household were identical figures on the census page. This was the case in 55 white and 41 black families in the 1900 sample.

15. See Appendix for age-specific death rates by race and sex and indices of dissimilarity and relative composition calculated from the number and percentages of deaths—1880 MS Census: Social Statistics, Virginia State Library, Richmond. The same calculations were made for all the deaths between 1864 and 1870 and the same was true for those years—Louisa Register of Deaths, 1864–1870, Louisa County, Va. Another indication that the Louisa record is inferior is contained in scattered state auditor's reports, which occasionally recorded deaths. Their totals were typically closer to the 1880 census enumeration totals. See *State Auditor's Report, 1896,* pp. 159–63, and *1898,* p. 211.

16. *Twelfth Census, 1900: Population,* vol. II, table 13, pp. 164–65. As late as 1961, the infant mortality rate for black children in McCormick County, S.C., was 107.3, proving that medical care in this affluent nation is still primarily for those who can afford it. See Robert Coles, *Migrants, Sharecroppers, Mountaineers,* vol. II of *Children of Crisis* (Boston: Little, Brown, 1971), 552. Mortality between the ages of one and ten was also striking, and in 1880, deaths of children (besides infants) in these young ages constituted the next highest percentage of all deaths. See Appendix.

17. See Appendix, esp. the index of relative composition.

18. Like the United States, Louisa's most common known causes of death were pneumonia, tuberculosis, and typhoid fever. Females were particularly susceptible to the type of tuberculosis known as scrofula. 1880 MS Census: Social Statistics.

19. Marriage Register. Marriages were sampled at three-year intervals between 1859 and 1901, except for blacks, for whom the sample began in 1865. Age, race, and sex constituted the data collected on all of the marriages in these three-year intervals. A total

of 86 white males remarried, compared with 22 white widows. These data may simply mean that widowed males were more likely to remarry. Since I do not known the actual number of the total widowed population by sex, these data alone would not confirm my hypothesis about greater male longevity, but taken together with age-specific death rates between 1864 and 1870 and 1880, data on the widowed lend greater support to the hypothesis. Also, recent studies have found widowers remarrying more often than widows by about 10 percent, which would not explain the much larger difference in Louisa. See Warren S. Thompson and P. K. Whelpton, *Population Trends in the United States,* vol. 9 (New York: Gordon and Breach, 1967), 206.

20. Gutman found that "large numbers of black women labored as field hands" *The Black Family,* 443 and n. 7, pp. 628–32.

21. See ch. 3, n. 11.

22. Based upon a one-in-ten sample (every tenth family) of the Louisa population from the Manuscript Census of Population of 1900. This recently opened census contains several useful categories of information not available in other censuses, among them one concerning the number of children ever borne by the mother.

NOTES TO CHAPTER VII

1. See Wiener, "Class Structure," 970–992.

2. Ransom and Sutch, *One Kind,* 186.

3. For evidence that black tenants were exploited in the credit market in the cotton South, see *ibid.,* 162–70.

4. Woodward, *The Strange Career.* Cf. Ransom and Sutch, *One Kind,* 195–97, and Gavin Wright, *The Political Economy of the Cotton South, Households, Markets, and Wealth in the Nineteenth Century* (New York: Norton, 1978), 186.

Bibliographical Essay

.

I used federal, state, and local records extensively for this study. How these records were used is the subject of the methodological appendix. In this essay I refer the reader to the primary and secondary sources which made my study possible and influenced its course.

The federal manuscript censuses of population and agriculture were indispensable. The population schedules included basic demographic and occupational information and the agricultural scheduels a wealth of detail on farm practices. The recently opened 1900 manuscript census of population added a column on the number of children borne by each mother, a valuable piece of information for demographic historians.

The use of federal censuses is not without problems, however. For example, manuscript censuses of 1890 (except for a few scattered counties) and the agricultural schedules for 1900 have been destroyed: 1890 by fire and 1900 due to a lack of official appreciation for their historical value. The census of 1860 enumerated the slave population separately and by first name, making it difficult, if not impossible, to link owners and slaves. Before 1880, researchers must infer the relationship of members of households. On the agricultural schedule of 1870 but not in subsequent years, enumerators provided the values of real estate and personal property for each household. Census values on land, livestock, machinery, fertilizer, labor, and production were determined by individual enumerators and therefore were highly subjective. I have used these figures with caution or substituted data from local tax records, where possible.

These are just a few of the problems which confront those who use the census. For a useful discussion of the problems, see Jonathan M. Wiener, "Appendix: The Manuscript Census," *Social Origins of the New South: Alabama, 1860–1885* (Baton Rouge: Louisiana State Univ. Press, 1978), 229–39. Problems of reliability and continuity notwithstanding, federal censuses remain a remarkably rich source of information for social historians. In the case of Virginia, they are widely available on microfilm from major university libraries of the state and from the Virginia State library.

The records of the field offices of the Bureau of Refugees, Freedmen and Abandoned lands, Records Group 105, housed at the National Archives, contain abundant material on economic and social conditions in the South between 1865 and 1869. In monthly reports from each county in the South, bureau officers reported on local conditions and submitted copies of labor contracts between landlords and tenants. The collection also contains policy statements of the bureau in the form of circulars, which flowed from the Washington headquarters of the agency to field representatives.

State records that provided data by county were scarce. Reports of the state auditor contained statistical information on land ownership and values per acre by race. More useful were the reports of the State Board of Agriculture on agricultural trends and labor conditions.

Local records at the Louisa Courthouse and the Virginia State Library in Richmond were as valuable as the federal records for this study. Land taxbooks made it possible to identify landowners, unlike the censuses, which focus upon operators. Personal property tax records were excellent sources on the remaining taxable wealth, including draft animals and livestock, farm implements, weapons, pianos, sewing machines, carriages, gold watches, and kitchen and household furniture. From these records, it was possible to determine the distribution of propertied wealth within Louisa County. When linked with federal census records, they made it possible to reconstruct the social history of Louisa's households and families.

Other courthouse records provided more specialized information. Deedbooks revealed the uses of property for credit or collateral, the operation of the lien system, and the customary practices of estate probation. Originally, I intended to link the information from these sources with other records, but this proved unfeasible and sampling techniques served just as well to explore general lien and probate practices. Demographic data were richer than I expected. The Louisa Marriage Register gave ages at marriage, occupation, and place of marriage by race and sex. County officials left an incomplete but useful record of births and deaths for the period 1865–71. A Crop Lien Docket and Delinquent List of Felons or Other Infamous Offenses since November 2nd, 1870 gave characteristic but incomplete accounts of debt and crime during the period.

The political history of Louisa was more difficult to piece together. Unfortunately, only three issues of the county newspaper were extant for the period 1865–1900, located at Alderman Library, the University of Virginia. These were nonetheless valuable for identifying local political leaders who could then be traced in local tax records. Especially useful were the minutes of the local governing body. The Board of Supervisors' Journal recorded the monthly decisions of this important political body regarding the collection and disbursement of county revenue and debates on controversial issues of local importance.

Private collections were not extensive but filled important gaps. The plantation records of Thomas S. Watson span the period. This large collection, which often contained correspondence between Watson and friends and relatives, illuminated the social, economic, and political views of these members of Louisa's economic elite. Although his business records did not follow disciplined bookeeping practices, they did supply some information on wage rates and labor conditions, relationships with former slaves, and especially his business activities outside agriculture. The ledger books of a local merchant and one-time slaveowner, Charles Danne, gave detailed information on local prices which affected household budgets. These records are housed at Alderman Library, the University of Virginia.

Among secondary sources, general tables of the census provided statistical snapshots of economic and social conditions at the ten-year intervals. Reports of the state auditor and the Board of Agriculture contributed statistical information regarding patterns in land ownership and agricultural trends. Donald J. Bogue and Calvin L. Beale, *Economic Areas of the United States* (Glencoe, Ill.: Free Press, 1961) sets economic realities of the 1950s and 1960s in an historical context of regional trends since the Civil War. Eugene M. Lerner, "Southern Output and Agricultural Income, 1860–1880," *Agricultural History* 33 (July 1959), 117–25 is of comparable importance. Everett S. Lee, *et al.*, *Population Redistribution and Economic Growth, United States, 1870–1880*, 3 vols. (Philadelphia: American Philosophical Society, 1957), and Warren S. Thompson and P. K. Whelpton, *Population Trends in the United States*, vol. 9 (New York: Gordon and Breach, 1967), are good references on demographic trends in the United States.

Agriculture in the United States has received extensive treatment. John T. Schlebecker, comp., *Bibliography of Books and Pamphlets on the History of Agriculture in the United States, 1607–1967* (Santa Barbara: American Bibliographical Center–Clio Press, 1969) is a bibliographical guide to this literature on the postwar South; see also Charles B. Dew, "Critical Essay on Recent Works," in C. Vann Woodward, *Origins of the New South, 1877–1913*, vol. IX of Wendell Holmes Stephenson and E. Merton Coulter, eds., *A History of the South* (Baton Rouge: Louisiana State Univ. Press, 1971), 591–96. General studies include Allan G. Bogue, *From Prairie to Corn Belt*

(Chicago: Univ. of Chicago Press, 1963); Paul W. Gates, *The Farmer's Age: Agriculture, 1815–1860,* vol. III, *The Economic History of the United States,* Henry David, *et al.,* eds. (New York: Harper and Row, 1960); and Fred A. Shannon, *The Farmer's Last Frontier: Agriculture 1860–1897,* vol. V, *The Economic History of the United States,* Henry David, *et al.,* eds. (New York: Farrar and Rinehart, 1945). Avery Craven, *Soil Exhaustion as a Factor in the Agricultural History of Virginia and Maryland, 1606–1860* (Urbana: Univ. of Illinois Press, 1926), deals with a special problem in southern agriculture. Robert Preston Brooks, *The Agrarian Revolution in Georiga, 1865–1912* (Westport, Conn.: Negro Univ. Press, 1970), and Enoch Marvin Banks, *The Economics of Land Tenure in Georgia* (New York: Columbia Univ. Press, 1905), provided good comparative material on landholding patterns in the rural South. Merle Curti, *The Making of an American Community: A Case Study of Democracy in a Frontier County* (Stanford: Stanford Univ. Press, 1959), was used to compare tenants and their conditions on the western frontier with southern tenants. Other more specialized studies are listed in the footnotes.

Extensive background reading in secondary sources is essential to placing local studies within the broader context of southern history. Too numerous to list completely, the general works I have found indispensable include the work of C. Vann Woodward mentioned above as well as his *Burden of Southern History* (Baton Rouge: Louisiana State Univ. Press, 1977); *Tom Watson, Agrarian Rebel* (New York: Oxford Univ. Press, 1969); *American Counterpoint, Slavery and Racism in the North-South Dialogue* (Boston: Little, Brown, 1971), esp. chs. 9–10; and *The Strange Career of Jim Crow* (New York: Oxford Univ. Press, 1974). Carl N. Degler, *The Other South: Southern Dissenters in the Nineteenth Century* (New York: Harper and Row, 1974), provides fresh perspectives on the period.

Virginius Dabney, *Virginia: The New Dominion; A History from 1607 to the Present* (Garden City, N. Y.: Doubleday, 1971), and Allen W. Moger, *Virginia: Bourbonism to Byrd, 1870–1925* (Charlottesville: Univ. Press of Virginia, 1968), are surveys of Virginia history with extensive bibliographies. Sheldon Hackney, "Origins of the New South in Retrospect" in *The Journal of Southern History,* 38 (May 1972), surveys the literature of the period since the publication of Woodward's *Origins* and should be consulted along with Charles Dew's "Critical Essay," listed above, for a comprehensive listing of secondary sources.

On racism as an ideological force, see George M. Frederickson, *The Black Image in the White Mind: The Debate on Afro-American Character and Destiny, 1817–1914* (New York: Harper and Row,

1971); Paul M. Gaston, *The New South Creed: A Study in Southern Mythmaking* (New York: Knopf, 1970); and W. J. Cash, *The Mind of the South* (New York: Vintage, 1941). On Cash and his critics, see C. Vann Woodward, "The Elusive Mind of the South," *American Counterpoint,* ch. 10. Clement Eaton, *The Freedom-of-Thought Struggle in the Old South* (New York: Harper and Row, 1964), shows how the defense of slavery developed in the South.

On slavery, especially as a system of race and class domination, see Eugene D. Genovese, *Roll, Jordon, Roll: The World the Slaves Made* (New York: Pantheon, 1974). See also his *In Red and Black: Marxian Explorations in Southern and Afro-American History* (New York: Vintage, 1971), esp. chs. 2, 3, 6, 8, and 15. Paul D. Escott, *Slavery Remembered: A Record of Twentieth-Century Slave Narratives* (Chapel Hill: Univ. of North Carolina Press, 1979), takes issue with Genovese's emphasis on paternalism. Peter H. Wood's *Black Majority: Negroes in Colonial South Carolina From 1670 Through the Stono Rebellion* (New York: Norton, 1974) does not cover the period of my study but influenced my thinking on slave culture and forms of resistance to white rule. Kenneth M. Stampp in *The Peculiar Institution: Slavery in the Ante-Bellum South* (New York: Vintage, 1956) challenged previous studies of slavery and it remains a standard work.

Recently, a debate on the black family has stimulated studies of this institution. Not available when I began my work, Herbert G. Gutman's *The Black Family in Slavery and Freedom 1750–1925* (New York: Random, 1977) is a thorough and overdue treatment which revises E. Franklin Frazier's *The Negro Family in the United States* (Chicago: Univ. of Chicago Press, 1939). See also Gutman, "Persistent Myths about the Afro-American Family," and Crandall A. Shifflett, "The Household Composition of Rural Black Families: Louisa County, Virginia, 1880," both in *Journal of Interdisciplinary History* 6, no. 2 *(The History of the Family* 3) (Autumn 1975) for discussions of the literature and further references. See also Charles S. Johnson, *Shadow of the Plantation* (Chicago: Univ. of Chicago Press, 1966), ch. II, and Peter Kolchin, *First Freedom: The Responses of Alabama's Blacks to Emancipation and Reconstruction* (Westport, Conn.: Greenwood, 1972), 56–78.

Social and economic studies of the Emancipation Period have at long last begun to correct the imbalance in the literature toward purely political studies. Leon Litwack's *Been in the Storm so Long: The Aftermath of Slavery* (New York: Vintage, 1980) also appeared as my work was nearing completion. It lends substantial weight to my arguments about the role of the Freedmen's Bureau and other state and local government policies in the economic subjugation of freedmen. Chapter 8 strengthens my contention that their economic dependency remained the source of race and class subordination, in spite of their "mania" to become landowners. See also James L. Roark, *Masters Without Slaves: Southern Planters in the Civil War and Reconstruction* (New York: Norton, 1977). For older but still useful background material on social and economic conditions, see Joel Williamson, *After Slavery: The Negro in South Carolina During Reconstruction, 1861–1877* (Chapel Hill: Univ. of North Carolina Press, 1965), and Roger W. Shugg, *Origins of Class Struggle in Louisiana: A Social History of White Farmers and Laborers during Slavery and After, 1840–1875* (Baton Rouge: Louisiana State Univ. Press, 1972).

A major conflict has grown in the literature over the Emancipation Period. Disagreement exists over the extent of economic progress and the explanations for economic growth and stagnation. Excellent summaries of the literature and lines of debate are available in Jonathan M. Wiener, "Class Structure and Economic Development in the American South, 1865–1955," including "Comments" by Robert Higgs and Harold D. Woodman and Wiener's "Reply," all in *American Historical Review*, 84, no. 4 (Oct. 1979), 970–1006, and Harold D. Woodman, "Sequel to Slavery: The New History Views the Postbellum South," *Journal of Southern History* 43, no. 4, (Nov. 1977), 523–54. One side argues from the theoretical base of free-enterprise capitalism. According to this view, freedmen made substantial economic progress after 1865; sharecropping, tenancy, and the lien system were market responses and benefited freedmen. Poverty and economic stagnation resulted from political interference with free market economy, such as occurred during the Reconstruction period when the Union government involved itself in southern politics. Racism also prevented the market from producing "optimal" results. The major exponents of these arguments include Robert Higgs, *The Transformation of the American Economy, 1865–1914: An Essay in Interpretation* (New York: Wiley, 1971), and *Competition and Coercion: Blacks in the American Economy, 1865–1914* (Cambridge: Cambridge Univ. Press, 1975); Joseph P. Reid, Jr. "Sharecropping as an Understandable Market Response: The Post-Bellum South," *Journal of Economic History*, 33 (Mar. 1973), 106–30; Stephen DeCanio, *Agriculture in the Postbellum South: The Economics of Production and Supply* (Cambridge, Mass.: MIT Press, 1974); Roger L. Ransom and Richard Sutch, *One Kind of Freedom: The Economic Consequences of Emancipation* (Cambridge: Cambridge Univ. Press, 1977). Further references to their work appear in Woodman and Wiener, above.

Historians have challenged the economic determinism of these so-called econometricians or cliometricians. In spite of a focus on the planter class, the contending argument is made from a Marxist theoretical base. According to this view, little progress was made among freedmen. Economic growth was limited by the "social origins" of planters, whose origins in the postwar South explain their actions after the Civil War. Sharecropping, tenancy, and the lien system were parts of "a repressive system of labor allocation and control." Planters rejected mechanization, diversification, and other progressive agricultural practices in favor of labor-intensive agriculture. See Jonathan M. Wiener, above, and his *Social Origins of the New South: Alabama, 1860–1885* (Baton Rouge: Louisiana State Univ. Press, 1978), 69, for the quote; Dwight Billings, Jr., *Planters and the Making of a "New South": Class, Politics, and Development in North Carolina 1865–1900* (Chapel Hill: Univ. of North Carolina Press, 1979); Jay Mandle, *The Roots of Black Poverty: The Southern Plantation Economy After the Civil War* (Durham: Duke Univ. Press, 1978), and Wiener and Woodman, above, for additional references.

The dispute over the Emancipation Period has raised questions which enabled me to clarify my own argument. Although I have taken issue with both sides, generally I have found the work of Wiener, Billings, and Mandle more helpful because of their understanding of the market as more than an economic institution.

Various sources treated the development of Virginia's public welfare system: Arthur W. James, *The Disappearance of the County Almshouse in Virginia* (Richmond: State Department of Public Welfare, 1926). Robert H. Kirkwood, *Fit Surroundings: District Homes Replace County Almshouses in Virginia* (Richmond: Virginia Department of Public Welfare, 1948); and Frank William Hoffer, *Counties in Transition: A Study of County Public and Private Welfare Administration in Virginia* (Charlottesville: Institute of Research in Social Sciences, Univ. of Virginia, 1929). Harriet L. Tynes, "History of Poor Relief Legislation in Virginia" (M.A. thesis, Univ. of Chicago, 1932) is a useful survey of legal landmarks in the development of Virginia's welfare system. The *First Annual Report of the State Board of Charities and Corrections* (Richmond: Superintendent of Public Printing, 1909) is a report on every almshouse in the state and the conditions in them. Virginia may be compared with national trends in David J. Rothman, *The Discovery of the Asylum* (Boston: Little, Brown, 1971) and Robert H. Bremner, *From the Depths: The Discovery of Poverty in the United States* (New York: New York Univ. Press, 1969).

Finally, sundry sources influenced my theoretical and methodological approaches. On measures of mobility and persistence and the importance of these questions, the work of Stephan Thernstrom has been helpful, esp. *Poverty and Progress: Social Mobility in a Nineteenth Century City* (New York: Atheneum, 1969); *The Other Bostonians:*

Poverty and Progress in the American Metropolis, 1880–1970. On paternalism and its relationship to capitalism in addition to the work of Eugene Genovese mentioned above, I have learned from E. P. Thompson, "Patrician Society, Plebian Culture," *Journal of Social History,* 7 (Summer 1974), 382–405, and *The Making of the English Working Class* (New York: Vintage, 1963), esp. 203–4 and 543–44. Karl Polanyi, *The Great Transformation* (Boston: Beacon, 1957), chs. 5–6; Max Weber, *The Protestant Ethic and the Spirit of Capitalism* (New York: Scribner's, 1958); Robert Brenner, "Agrarian Class Structure and Economic Development in Pre-Industrial Europe," *Past and Present* 70 (1976), 30–75; and Barrington Moore, Jr., *Social Origins of Dictatorship and Democracy: Lord and Peasant in the Making of the Modern World* (Boston: Beacon, 1966), chs. 3 and 7–9.

Much can be learned about resistance, individual and collective, and the conditions which favor or dampen it by studying peasant society. The literature is vast, but most useful were E. J. Hobsbawm, *Primitive Rebels* (New York: Norton, 1965); Hobsbawm and George Rudé, *Captain Swing* (New York: Pantheon, 1968); Roland Mousnier, *Peasant Uprisings in Seventeenth-Century France, Russia, and China,* trans. Brian Pearce (New York: Harper and Row, 1970); Karl Marx, *The Eighteenth Brumaire of Louis Bonaparte* (New York: International, 1963), esp. 123–24; Charles Tilly, "Collective Violence in European Perspective," in Hugh Davis Graham and Ted Robert Gurr, eds., *Violence in America: Historical and Comparative Perspectives,* (New York: Bantam, 1969), 4–45; and Charles, Louis, and Richard Tilly, *The Rebellious Century, 1830–1930* (Cambridge, Mass.: Harvard Univ. Press, 1975).

My understanding of agricultural production as a function of yield-producing factors comes from my reading of Theodore W. Schultz, *Transforming Traditional Agriculture* (New Haven: Yale Univ. Press, 1964).

On conceptual approaches to family history, a sampling of the many theoretical arguments which I have found helpful include Meyer Fortes, "The Developmental Cycle in Domestic Groups," in Jack Goody, ed., *Kinship* (Baltimore: Penguin, 1971), 85–98; Talcott Parsons, "The Kinship System of the Contemporary United States," in Parsons, ed., *Essays in Sociological Theory* (New York: Free Press, 1954); Michael Anderson, "The Study of Family Structure," in E. A. Wrigley, ed., *Nineteenth Century Society* (Cambridge: Cambridge Univ. Press, 1972), 47–81; Peter Laslett, "Mean Household Size in England Since the Sixteenth Century," in Laslett and Richard Wall, eds., *Household and Family in Past Time* (Cambridge: Cambridge Univ. Press, 1972), 125–58; Raymond T. Smith, "The Nuclear Family in Afro-American Kinship," *Journal of Comparative Fami-*

ly Studies 1 (Autumn 1970), 55–70; Yonina Talmon-Garber, "Social Change and Family Structure," in Bernard Farber, ed., *Kinship and Family Organization* (New York: Wiley, 1966), 88–101; and Norman E. Whitten, Jr., and John F. Szwed, "Introduction," in Whitten and Szwed, eds., *Afro-American Anthropology* (New York: Free Press, 1970), 23–53.

On the relationship between family and economy, of great help to me were Eric R. Wolf, *Peasants* (Englewood Cliffs, N. J.: Prentice-Hall, 1966), chs. 2–3; A. V. Chayanov, *The Theory of Peasant Economy,* ed. Daniel Thorner, Basile Kerblay, and R. E. F. Smith (Homewood, Ill.: Richard D. Irwin, 1966), esp. 53–69; Lutz K. Berkner, "The Stem Family and the Developmental Cycle of the Peasant Household: An Eighteenth Century Austrian Example," *American Historical Review* 77, no. 2 (Apr. 1972), 398–418; H. J. Habbakuk, "Family Structure and Economic Change in Nineteenth Century Europe," *Journal of Economic History* 15 (1955), 1–12; Michael Anderson, *Family Structure in Nineteenth Century Lancashire* (London: Cambridge Univ. Press, 1971); Peter Laslett, *The World We Have Lost* (New York: Scribner's, 1965); Michael Young and Peter Willmott, *Family and Kinship in East London* (Baltimore; Penguin, 1971). Further references on work in family history may be found in Michael Gordon, ed., *The American Family in Social-Historical Perspective* (New York: St. Martin's Press, 1978) and in various issues of *Family History,* Tamara Hareven, editor.

Finally, on the relationship of racism to the social structure, see Harold Wolpe, "Industrialism and Race in South Africa," and John Rex, "The Concept of Race in Sociological Theory," both in Sami Zubaida, ed., *Race and Racialism* (New York and London: Tavistock, 1970).

Index

.

Patronage and Poverty in the Tobacco South is set in ten point Garamond type with one and one-half point spacing between the lines. Garamond is also used for display. The book was designed by Jim Billingsley. The book was composed by Williams of Chattanooga, Tennessee, printed by Thomson-Shore, Inc., Dexter, Michigan, and bound by John H. Dekker & Sons, Grand Rapids, Michigan. The paper on which the book is printed bears the watermark of S.D. Warren and is designed for an effective life of at least three hundred years.

THE UNIVERSITY OF TENNESSEE PRESS : KNOXVILLE